THE FOUNDATION OF BIBLICAL AUTHORITY

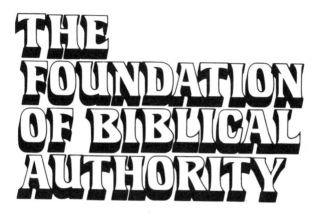

THE FOUNDATION OF BIBLICAL AUTHORITY

FRANCIS A. SCHAEFFER

JOHN H. GERSTNER
R.C. SPROUL

JAMES I. PACKER
JAMES MONTGOMERY BOICE

GLEASON L. ARCHER
KENNETH S. KANTZER

Edited by
James Montgomery Boice

ZONDERVAN
PUBLISHING HOUSE
OF THE ZONDERVAN CORPORATION
GRAND RAPIDS, MICHIGAN 49506

THE FOUNDATION OF BIBLICAL AUTHORITY

Copyright © 1978 by The Zondervan Corporation
Grand Rapids, Michigan

Library of Congress Cataloging in Publication Data
Main entry under title:

The Foundation of Biblical authority.

   1. Bible—Evidences, authority, etc. I. Schaeffer,
Francis August. II. Boice, James Montgomery, 1938-
BS480.F68   220.1'3   78-12801
ISBN 0-310-21521-8

Printed in the United States of America

The chapter by Kenneth S. Kantzer, "Evangelicals and the Doctrine of Inerrancy," is adapted from *Evangelical Roots*, edited by Kenneth S. Kantzer (Nashville: Thomas Nelson and Sons, 1978) and is used by permission. It has also appeared in an adapted form in *Christianity Today* (April 21, 1978).

To Him
whose Word will never pass away

CONTENTS

Preface

THE INTERNATIONAL COUNCIL ON BIBLICAL INERRANCY

THIS VOLUME is the first scholarly production of a new organization of pastors, professors, and Christian laymen: The International Council on Biblical Inerrancy. Founded in 1977, after a year of careful conversations and planning, the ICBI has as its purpose the defense and application of the doctrine of biblical inerrancy as an essential element for the authority of Scripture and a necessity for the health of the church. It was created to counter the drift from this important doctrinal foundation by significant segments of evangelicalism and the outright denial of it by other church movements. At one of its early meetings, the Council adopted the following statement as an expression of its purpose.

The Situation

1. Even among evangelicals, Christian doctrine and Christian living are moving progressively away from the Bible's standard and from the classical teachings of the church.

2. This tragic departure is directly related to the denial in many quarters of the historical doctrine of the verbal inerrancy of the Bible.

3. Large portions of evangelical scholarship, which have accepted many of the negative critical theories of the writing of the Bible and a neo-orthodox approach to revelation, are endeavoring to redefine evangelicalism after their own image.

4. Most laymen, Christian leaders, and pastors seem to be theologically unequipped to discern this departure from the historic view of the Bible or to see the vast consequences which tend to follow from that departure.

5. Because of a contemporary unbiblical view of love and a low evaluation of truth, many evangelicals who are alerted to this doctrinal departure tend optimistically to think the problem will somehow vanish. Or they find themselves emotionally resistant to any effort to have the issues clarified, which might result in referring to some brothers and sisters as unbiblical.

"Peace at any cost" is the emotional position of vast numbers of evangelicals in the 1970s. This attitude complicates the matter of "speaking the truth in love" because many evangelicals think that "speaking the truth" means one cannot be "speaking in love" when certain issues or persons are involved.

In light of the situation we see, and in response to the burden it has placed on our hearts, we commit to writing the purpose to which we now commit ourselves:

Our Purpose

To take a united stand in elucidating, vindicating, and applying the doctrine of biblical inerrancy as an essential element for the authority of Scripture and a necessity for the health of the church of God, and to attempt to win the church back to this historic position.

Our Objectives

1. To host a meeting of carefully chosen evangelical leaders, all of whom are committed to the biblical doctrine of inerrancy.

2. To create and publish a clear statement on inerrancy endorsed by a united coalition of prominent evangelical scholars, declaring therein that the Bible is true not only in matters of faith and practice but also in other matters such as statements relating to history and science.

3. To stimulate the communication and application of the concept of biblical inerrancy both in the academic theological community and at a popular level.

Plans for the International Council on Biblical Inerrancy for the next ten years involve two major thrusts: academic defense of the inerrancy position and practical Christian instruction. Academic work will lay the foundation needed for the church to proceed on the basis of a Bible that is true in whatever it touches. Work will be done in the areas of biblical, historical, theological, and philosophical studies and practical theology. Instruction will be offered to pastors, Christian workers and lay persons regarding inerrancy and related issues. On the drawing board is a national network of training centers for those who are committed to an inerrant Bible and who are eager to join hands across denominational and theological lines to defend and advance this position.

Some will charge those who hold to inerrancy with making mountains out of molehills and with dividing the evangelical church. Members of the Council believe that they are simply calling a mountain a mountain and think it reasonable to expect that the ICBI will be a unifying force within evangelicalism, as it encourages Christian brothers and sisters to stand for the only objective foundation of a sure revelation from God there is—inerrancy.

Still other persons will argue that *infallibility* is a better word than *inerrancy* for describing the soundest evangelical position on Scripture and will wish that the ICBI were called the International Council on Biblical Infallibility instead. As some use this word, the choice of infallible would probably be acceptable. They recognize that in order for the Bible to be infallible in its truest and fullest extent it must be inerrant. Unfortunately, the majority of those who choose infallible rather than inerrant do so because they want to affirm something less than total inerrancy, suggesting erroneously that the Bible is dependable in some areas (such as faith and morals) while not being fully dependable in others (such as matters of history and science). Because of this situation and because of its commitment to total inerrancy, the ICBI has chosen to name itself by the use of the stronger word.

Although a firm stand on God's propositional truth will be taken by each ICBI member, the Council trusts the church will not see it repeating the harshness characteristic of some who defended the position in the 1920s and 1930s. The Council assumes that evangelicals committed to inerrancy will continue to work hand in hand with all other evangelicals for such common causes as world evangelization and hunger relief, and against such common foes as liberalism, the occult, moral permissiveness, and abortion on demand. The ICBI thus hopes to foster "a coalition within a coalition" and believes that an inner coalition of evangelicals who hold to inerrancy will be a "hard core" providing strength for evangelicalism as a whole. It believes that without this core evangelicalism will eventually crumble and fall under increasing pressures coming upon it from secular culture.

The executive council of the ICBI is composed of the following members: Gleason L. Archer, James M. Boice, Edmund P. Clowney, Norman L. Geisler, John H. Gerstner, Jay H. Grimstead, Harold W. Hoehner, Don E. Hoke, A. Wetherell Johnson, Kenneth S. Kantzer, James I. Packer, J. Barton Payne, Robert D. Preus, Earl D. Radmacher, Francis A. Schaeffer, and R.C. Sproul.

The advisory board currently consists of Jay E. Adams, John W. Alexander, Hudson T. Armerding, Greg L. Bahnsen, Henri A.G. Blocher, William R. Bright, W.A. Criswell, Robert K. DeVries, Charles L. Feinberg, William N. Garrison, D. James Kennedy, Jay L. Kesler, Fred H. Klooster, George W. Knight, Harold B. Kuhn, Samuel R. Külling, Gordon R. Lewis, Harold Lindsell, John F. MacArthur, Josh P. McDowell, Allan A. McRae, Walter A. Maier, Roger R. Nicole, Harold J. Ockenga, Raymond C. Ortlund, Luis Palau, Adrian P. Rogers, Lorne C. Sanny, Robert L. Saucy, Frederick R. Schatz, Joseph R. Schultz, Morton H. Smith, Ray C. Stedman, G. Aiken Taylor, Merrill C. Tenney, Larry L. Walker, and John F. Walvoord.

Evangelicals who are interested in the Council and its work may write to: The International Council on Biblical Inerrancy, P. O. Box 13261, Oakland, California 94611.

Forty years ago the issues were clearer than they are today. Those who rejected the classical, historical view of the Bible at that time tended to fall into obvious heresies, such as rejecting the deity of Christ or the necessity of the Atonement. Today, since the existential method of viewing truth has come into theology, the situation is different. Now some evangelical scholars do not feel at all embarrassed to build a house of evangelical doctrine on the foundation of a liberal or neoorthodox view of Scripture.

Based on the academic work of its scholars, the goal of the ICBI is to help lead the average evangelical to a point of mature decision-making ability by offering a reasoned defense of the highest possible view of Scripture: what the Bible says, God says—through human agents and without error.

James Montgomery Boice
Philadelphia, Pennsylvania

GOD GIVES HIS PEOPLE
A SECOND OPPORTUNITY

Foreword: Francis A. Schaeffer

Francis A. Schaeffer is the founder of L'Abri Fellowship in the village of Heumoz in the Swiss Alps. L'Abri has branches in Italy, France, Holland, and Great Britain. For ten years prior to his work in Switzerland he was a pastor in the United States. He is the author of The God Who Is There; Escape From Reason; He Is There and He is Not Silent; Death in the City; Pollution and the Death of Man; The Church at the End of the Twentieth Century; The Mark of the Christian; The Church Before the Watching World; True Spirituality; Basic Bible Studies; Genesis in Space and Time; The New Super-Spirituality; Back to Freedom and Dignity; Art and the Bible; No Little People; Two Contents, Two Realities; Joshua and the Flow of Biblical History; No Final Conflict; Everybody Can Know *(with Edith Schaeffer); and* How Should We Then Live? *The last-named book is also available as a ten-part film-and-television series. Dr. Schaeffer holds the following degrees: Hampden-Sydney College, A.B.; Faith Theological Seminary, B.D.; and Gordon College, LL.D.*

Foreword: Francis A. Schaeffer

GOD GIVES HIS PEOPLE A SECOND OPPORTUNITY

W HAT WE have known as evangelicalism stands in chaos in the second half of the 1970s. What our children and grandchildren will have, if Christ does not return, depends on making the right, though difficult, choices that face us at this time.

While reviewing Carl Henry's book *Evangelicals in Search of Identity*, Richard Quebedeaux, author of *The Young Evangelicals*, says, "Evangelicals used to be easy to identify. . . . They believed that the Bible is inerrant because it is God's inspired Word, and God cannot lie or contradict himself. . . . But no longer. Since the emergence of the young evangelicals. . . ."[1] This defines the problem and shows where evangelicalism now stands in regard to the Bible. It is so accurate that one must wonder if the word *evangelical* will have meaning for much longer.

What is the historic background of all this? I would like to write my own conviction regarding the historic flow that is one of the factors bringing us to where we are in the 1970s.

In the 1930s Bible-believing Christians were united on a wide front. The old, preexistential liberalism was rising like a flood in most of the old-line denominations in the United States. Bible-believing Christians over a wide front agreed that this had to be met clearly. The old *Sunday School Times* under Philip E. Howard, Sr., and Charles G. Trumbull is a good example of a clear voice in a journal. The scholar who best represented this clear and united

15

stand against the rapidly growing liberalism in both the bureauc-
racies of the old-line denominations and in the seminaries was
J. Gresham Machen. But other scholars in many denominations
and many less-well-known people were united. Those united
across many denominations for Bible-believing Christianity
spoke of the fundamentals of the faith in contrast to the liberals'
flood of pronouncements. They did not see inerrancy as an "ism"
but for what it was—the historic Christian position; that is, that
the Bible is God's Word, without error in all the areas of which it
speaks. "All areas," and not just religious matters!

This was one of the points classical Roman Catholicism and the
Reformation churches had in common and continued to have in
common in the United States until the old liberalism took over in
most of the Protestant denominations and seminaries between
1900 and the 1930s. (Later, after Vatican II, it became apparent
that many Roman Catholic theologians also no longer hold what
had always been the classical Roman Catholic view of the Bible.)
Kirsopp Lake, no friend of the historic Bible-believing position,
wrote:

> It is a mistake often made by educated persons who happen to have
> but little knowledge of historical theology to suppose that fun-
> damentalism is a new and strange form of thought. It is nothing of
> the kind; it is the partial and uneducated survival of a theology
> which was once universally held by all Christians. How many were
> there, for instance, in Christian churches in the eighteenth century
> who doubted the infallible inspiration of all Scripture? A few,
> perhaps, but very few. No, the fundamentalist may be wrong; I
> think that he is. But it is we who have departed from the tradition,
> not he; and I am sorry for the fate of anyone who tries to argue with
> a fundamentalist on the basis of authority. The Bible and the *corpus
> theologicum* of the Church are on the fundamentalist side.[2]

F.C. Grant, who taught at Union Seminary of New York, wrote in
regard to the writers of the New Testament in his *Introduction to
New Testament Thought:*

> Everywhere it is taken for granted that what is written in Scripture
> is the work of divine inspiration, and therefore trustworthy, infalli-
> ble, and inerrant. . . . No New Testament writer would dream of
> questioning a statement contained in the Old Testament.[3]

To try to relate the Bible-believing position to something beginning only in the United States around 1900 simply is not to
read the history of the church. Carl Henry is eminently right

when, in an interview in *Eternity* magazine, he said in regard to inerrancy: "It was Jesus' view, and that of the apostles, and of the church fathers, and of the Roman Catholic Church down to Vatican II. The recent effort to detach the Reformers from that view, and to place them on the side of scriptural errancy, is unpersuasive."[4]

In the 1930s, Bible-believing Christians across all denominational lines were united in confessing that the Bible is "not partly true and partly false, but all true, the blessed, holy Word of God—this warm and vital type of Christianity," as Machen put it.[5] Unhappily the old liberals gained control of the bureacracies and seminaries of most of the old-line denominations.

At this point a tragedy occurred that is a part of the seedbed of our situation in the 1970s. Most Bible-believing Christians divided into two groups: 1) those who held to the purity of the visible church and felt the various old-line denominations had passed the point of reclamation and left those denominations, and 2) those who either gave up the concept of the purity of the visible church or thought their denominations could be reclaimed.

I represent the first group, for I left my denomination at that time and have stressed what I believe is the biblical position of the purity of the visible church ever since. Good things came out of this group, but I believe two things have minimized its influence even to the present day. First, when the men and women of this group left their denominations, many felt that those who stayed in had betrayed them; unhappily they then spent more time fighting (I choose the word sadly but carefully) the Bible-believing Christians who stayed in than standing against the liberals. Standing for the Word of God got lost in harshness and looking inward to such an extent that gradually some who still held as strongly as ever to the principle of the purity of the visible church felt that things were being done and said that negated the possibility of standing for the position of the purity of the visible church before reasonable men and women. These withdrew from what had come to be called "the separated movement," though continuing to maintain denominations and seminaries that taught and practiced the purity of the visible church.

Second, some who held to the principle of the purity of the visible church put (it seems to me) the chasm at the wrong point. They made absolute division at the point of their distinctives— Reformed theology, believers' baptism, a Lutheran view of the sacraments, etc.—rather than between those who were Bible-believing Christians and those who were not, and then practicing their distinctives carefully on *this* side of the chasm.

So much for the weaknesses of those who left the liberal denominations.

But now, what about the other side, those who sought to follow a broader way? Many good things came out of this group also. But in the 1970s problems are evident. It is always difficult to take a broader way without the next generation carrying that broader way into a latitudinarianism of doctrine, especially a latitudinarianism concerning the Bible. This drift has occurred, and at the present time certain schools and individuals are attempting to make all evangelicalism over into a movement embracing their own view of the Bible—a view that the "broader group" in the 1930s would never have accepted. A leader of the broader group in the 1930s recently put the matter to me like this: "There are two points. First, I hate to see the movement divided. Second, anyone is naive not to see that the movement is already divided and that we did not divide it but that it was divided by those who have changed their view of Scripture."

So here we are, both sides flowing out of the situation in the 1930s. And if I am right, we have only a short time to save an appreciable part of evangelicalism from the "slippery slope," as one British journal called it.

How can we save it? I think we should see that at this moment God is giving his people a second opportunity. This time can be an optimistic, positive one. To take this opportunity means going back to the 1930s and picking up the pieces from the mistakes that were made then. It should be seen as an opportunity from God and not as a moment for despair or just drifting.

Those on both sides who continue to hold to the historic view concerning the Bible should say "I'm sorry" where it is needed. Both sides should let history be history and not reopen the old sores, except to learn not to repeat the same mistakes in an even more complicated and subtle age. The broader group should realize that a line must be drawn with love, yet drawn. The other side should realize that harshness is not to be confused with standing for holiness and that in an age like our own, surrounded by a relativistic culture and by a relativistic church, which bends the Bible to the changing whims of this age, the chasm should be kept in the right place, with all our strongly believed-in distinctives on this side of the chasm, rather than making the distinctives the chasm.

None of us should want the ugliness of the 1930s repeated. We who stand for the Word of God as without mistake not only when it speaks of salvation matters but also when it speaks of the cosmos, history, and moral norms, must be careful to live under the Word we say we hold dear, and that very much includes love to those (many of whom are certainly brothers and sisters in Christ) who we think are at this time making a dreadful and destructive mistake in their view of the Bible. But love and personal fellowship does not mean allowing this view of the Bible to shape the next generation. If it does, the next generation will be swept away, and the church of Christ will have lost the absolute by which to judge or help the relativistic surrounding culture. Also, those who are taking the new view of Scripture tend to distract those who hold the historic view of a Bible that is without mistake when it speaks of history and the cosmos, as well as when it speaks of salvation, from a very real task that confronts them: a careful and prayerful determination as to what extent a Cartesian, positivistic,.empiricist mentality has influenced the exegesis of that inerrant Bible. This is a task that should be confronting our scholars and seminaries. Those who are trying to use such questions as a springboard to force their own existential methodology on all evangelicalism must not distract us from it.

It must also be said lovingly that those who hold the new view of Scripture are not automatically free from the danger of a lack of love, as is shown by some of the things written by them. But that is their responsibility before God.

Those who continue to hold that the Bible is without mistake because it is God's inspired Word and that God cannot lie or contradict himself have a responsibility before God to take advantage of the second opportunity he has given us—to pick up the pieces all the way back to the 1930s. By the grace of God we must do better in order to stand in our generation with love, but with total clarity, for a Bible "not partly true and partly false, but all true, the blessed, holy Word of God—this warm and vital type of Christianity."

Notes

[1]Richard Quebedeaux, in a review of the book *Evangelicals in Search of Identity*, *Radix* magazine (May-June 1977), p. 14.

[2]Kirsopp Lake, *The Religion of Yesterday and Tomorrow* (Boston: Houghton, 1926), p. 61.

[3]Frederick C. Grant, *An Introduction to New Testament Thought* (New York: Abingdon-Cokesbury, 1950), p. 75.

[4]Carl F.H. Henry, "The House Divided: An Interview with Carl Henry," *Eternity* (October 1976), p. 38.

[5]J. Gresham Machen, *The Attack Upon Princeton Seminary: A Plea for Fair Play* (Philadelphia: Johnson and Prince, 1927), p. 37.

THE CHURCH'S DOCTRINE
OF BIBLICAL INSPIRATION

John H. Gerstner

John H. Gerstner is Professor of Church History, Pittsburgh Theological Seminary, Pittsburgh, Pennsylvania, and Visiting Professor, Trinity Evangelical Divinity School, Deerfield, Illinois. He is a graduate of Westminster College, B.D.; Westminster Theological Seminary, B.Th., M.Th.; and Harvard University, Ph.D. He holds honorary degrees from Tarkio College, D.D.; and Westminster College, L.H.D. Among his many articles and books are: Calvin's Political Influence in the United States, The Epistle to the Ephesians, The Gospel According to Rome, An Inerrancy Primer, A Predestination Primer, Reasons for Faith, A Reconciliation Primer, Steps to Salvation: A Study in the Evangelistic Message of Jonathan Edwards, Survey of the Cults, Theology for Everyman, Theology of the Major Sects, *"Warfield's Case for Biblical Inerrancy" in* God's Inerrant Word, *edited by John Warwick Montgomery, and "The Message of the Word" in* The Bible: The Living Word of Revelation, *edited by Merrill C. Tenney. Dr. Gerstner is a contributing editor for* Christianity Today. *He is a member of the Evangelical Theological Society, the American Church History Society, and the American Theological Libraries Association. Earlier in his career he held two pastorates in western Pennsylvania.*

1 *John H. Gerstner*

THE CHURCH'S DOCTRINE OF BIBLICAL INSPIRATION

THE REASON for the title of this book on inerrancy, *The Foundation of Biblical Authority*, is plain: The Bible's being the Word of God is the *only* foundation for full *biblical authority*.[1] If the Bible is not the Word of God, it has no divine authority. We realize that some who disagree with inerrancy are claiming inspiration for parts of the Bible, the so-called salvation parts. Very well, but then they cannot title their position *biblical authority* but only *partial biblical authority*. To add insult to injury to God's Word, they cannot tell precisely what parts of the Bible are inspired. They say "salvation parts," but they do not tell us where to find these or how to separate them from the uninspired, errant, nonsalvation parts.

Many modern biblical scholars contend that there are different salvation schemes in the Bible.[2] Thus, partial biblical authority, however sincerely advocated, becomes the road to the destruction of even partial biblical authority. Advocates of this position are worse off than those who look for a needle in a haystack, because a needle in a haystack can be found!

Furthermore, some evangelical scholars not only favor partial biblical authority today but believe that the historic Christian church believed it. Our attempt in this essay will be to show that the main historic path has been *total biblical authority*. It is significant that the current fourth edition of *The New Columbia Ency-*

23

clopedia[3] recognizes this. While this most massive and comprehensive one-volume encyclopedia in the world possesses a great deal of religious information, it is essentially secular in viewpoint and quite objective. Its matter-of-fact statement is therefore all the more impressive:

> The traditional Christian view of the Bible is that it was *all* written under the guidance of God and that it is, therefore, *all true,* literally or under the veil of allegory. *In recent times,* however, the view of many Protestants has been influenced by the pronouncements of critics (see Higher Criticism). This has produced a counter-reaction in the form of Fundamentalism, whose chief emphasis has been on the inerrancy of the Bible (italics added).[4]

The traditional Christian view is that the Bible is "all true." What "Fundamentalism" has reacted to is deviation from the historic norm.

Laymen especially are puzzled that experts differ about this matter of the church's historic position on inerrancy. Why do men who have studied the subject thoroughly come so often to differing and even conflicting conclusions, and how can lay people understand the matter if the scholars maintain exactly opposite interpretations of the very same data?

This is not so difficult to answer as it may appear. The trouble is very rarely in the sources of information. It is usually in the deductions that are drawn from the sources. Some scholars of massive learning are not so skilled in drawing conclusions. Some laymen who know nothing of the subject matter, except what the experts tell them, can easily see that certain conclusions drawn by the experts do not follow from the data presented by the experts. Thus, they may be benefited by the scholar's learning and not be harmed by his *non sequiturs.*

There are five very common *non sequiturs* (things that do not follow) in the field we are about to survey. If the reader will master them, he will, we believe, avoid a great deal of misunderstanding.

1. The phenomenal *non sequitur*
2. The accommodation *non sequitur*
3. The emphasis *non sequitur*
4. The critical *non sequitur*
5. The docetist *non sequitur*

The *phenomenal non sequitur:* the Bible's representing things as they *appear* (phenomena) has occasioned the logical leap that it contains error, because that is not the way things *are.* Obviously, this does not follow. If the Bible taught that things appeared one way and they did not appear that way, that would be an error. Or, if the Bible taught that things were one way and they were not that way, that would also be an error. But, for the Bible to teach that things appear one way when they actually are another way is not error. A simple illustration is assuming that the Bible is in error when it refers to a "sunrise" (which is how things appear) because that is not the way things are (the sun does not "rise").[5]

The *accommodation non sequitur:* the Bible's representing God as accommodating himself to human language has occasioned the logical leap that his Word contains error, because accommodation to human language involves accommodation to human error. Obviously, this is also not right. It does not follow that because God accommodates himself to human language he must accommodate himself to human error. An example is the supposition that the Bible's representing God as "repenting" (which is how it represents the matter to us) is an error because of God's unchangeableness (which is how it is).[6]

The *emphasis non sequitur:* the Bible's emphasizing certain things has occasioned the logical leap that it contains error, because it must be indifferent to other unemphasized things. But it does not follow that because the Bible stresses one thing, it errs in the things it does not stress. For example, it does not follow from the Bible's stress on salvation that it may err in mere historical details.[7]

The *critical non sequitur:* the fact that theologians perform the work of textual critics has occasioned the logical leap that they believe the Bible contains error. But it does not follow that because a scholar examines a text to see whether it belongs to the Bible he therefore believes the Bible can err. For example, questioning whether the doxology to the Lord's Prayer is in the original text of the Bible does not imply that the Bible itself can be in error.[8]

The *docetic non sequitur:* the Bible's representing itself as the Word of God written by men has occasioned the logical leap that it is therefore errant. Obviously this too does not follow. It does not follow that since God inspired men, he would be incapable of keeping them free of human error in writing. For example, it does not follow from the Bible's saying that God used Paul in the writing of epistles that God could not keep those epistles free from human error.[9]

Equipped with this logical Geiger counter to detect hidden mines and booby traps, let us tread our way carefully, though hastily, through the path of history in an attempt to ascertain "the church's doctrine of biblical inspiration."[10]

THE EARLY CHURCH

As we come to the teaching of the early church on inspiration, a word about the philosophical background of this period is in order. The two greatest philosophers of Greek antiquity were Plato and Aristotle. But Plato had far greater influence than Aristotle on the early church ever since the days of Justin Martyr, the converted Platonist philosopher. Although Aristotle gave the stronger argument for creation and freedom, he was ignored apparently because of the detachedness of his "First Mover" deity and the fatalism of his providence. Plato, on the other hand, was more mystical and disposed toward revelation, and his philosophical idealism was warmer.

The fundamental difference between Plato and Aristotle was not so much epistemological (pertaining to the way of knowing), however, as metaphysical (pertaining to what is known). Both believed in the apprehension of sensory data by the mind. But Plato believed that the "universals" or "ideas" thus apprehended exist independently, whereas Aristotle taught that they exist only in regard to or in connection with the thing apprehended. Augustine, in whom the Platonic element reached its ecclesiastical peak,[11] and Aquinas, in whom Aristotelianism did, entertained their mentors' differences about the universals but did not differ essentially on the way of knowing. Neither was fideistic in the sense of being unrational, irrational, or antirational. Aquinas believed an act of faith was necessary to appropriate revealed truth, and Augustine believed that faith in God and Scripture had to be rationally "worthy of belief."

The apostolic fathers and the apologists who span the second century clearly taught the Bible's own doctrine about the Bible, namely, inerrancy. W. Colkins has well summarized with full documentation that stance of the apostolic fathers, who lived during the first half of the second century—that is, immediately following the period of the apostles themselves:

> These fathers bear direct testimony to three of St. Paul's Epistles and indicate his inspiration. A few passages of the New Testament are distinctly quoted either as the language of the Lord, the Apos-

tles, or of "Scripture." . . . There are many expressions apparently taken from the New Testament; also allusions and references too inexact to be called quotations, which singly appear insignificant but occurring on every page are weighty arguments.[12]

Thus the apostolic father Clement of Rome, who is as explicit as any other of these fathers, writes of the Scriptures that they are "sayings of the Holy Spirit" and sayings "through the Holy Spirit," citing such Bible remarks as "the Holy Spirit says."[13] It has been said that Papias tended to depreciate the written Word in favor of oral tradition,[14] but this was only because he was collecting oral tradition and not because he did not respect and reverence the written Word.

The apologists of the second half of the second century and later are even more explicit than the apostolic fathers. Some of their language suggests "mechanical" inspiration, though apparently they did not believe that doctrine. We find Justin Martyr calling God the "plectrum" and the biblical writers the "lyre."[15] Athenagoras uses the simile of the flute.[16] Theophilus speaks of Moses writing the law but checks himself, saying, "Rather, the Word of God through him."[17] Tatian writes to the same effect.[18] But it is to be remembered, as Miltiades pointed out, that it was not necessary for prophets to be in a state of ecstacy.[19] Thus, the apologists may not have meant to teach mechanical inspiration, but there can be no mistaking that they held to divine, inerrant inspiration.

The apostolic fathers and the apologists were Eastern fathers, but in the newly developing Western church the same doctrine about the Bible was being promulgated. Irenaeus used the phrase "the Holy Spirit says"[20] as did Cyprian.[21] Tertullian was the most theologically articulate of all, saying not only that every writing of Scripture was useful (as against Marcion, who was trying to exclude the Old Testament and restrict the New Testament canon to Pauline Epistles) but also that the Scriptures were the "words," "letters," and very "voice of God."[22]

The most erudite scholar of the early church was Origen. For him, inspiration extended even to the iota of Scripture and the letters.[23] Scripture contained no faults, being "Spirit-inspired." He added that this doctrine of infallibility was taught in all the churches.[24]

In *Biblical Authority* Jack Rogers acknowledges that for Origen "the Bible was harmonious throughout and 'supernaturally perfect in every particular.'" But, he continues, "at the same time, Origen was very conscious of the human character of the holy writings [note *non sequitur* no. 5]. He knew that the New Testament was not written in the best Greek. But to him, that was unimportant because the revelation did not consist in the words but in the things revealed"[25] (note *non sequitur* no. 3). We have noted above that Origen insisted that the revelation did consist in words, even in letters. God simply used the best words inerrantly to communicate his message; he even used bad Greek if that was the Greek his audience understood. In this same section Rogers misunderstands Origen's use of "accommodation." When Origen represents God as revealing himself "like a schoolmaster talking 'little language' to his children," he is not for a moment suggesting that language is unimportant *(non sequitur* no. 2). Just the opposite. Language is so important that God condescends to "baby talk" in order to be understood verbally. The significance of divine accommodation is misunderstood by Rogers not only in Origen but also in Chrysostom (d. 407),[26] who, incidentally, was also a strong advocate of verbal inspiration, frequently calling the mouth of the prophet the "mouth of God."[27] We note that Vawter believed that Origen did not regard the Bible as the work of men but of God[28] and that he tried to resist the dictation doctrine.[29]

For lack of space I will not spell out the similar doctrines of Ambrose, Jerome,[30] and a host of other teachers of the early church, nor will I deny that there was rare dissent among some early fathers in regard to inerrancy.

Speaking generally, the early church held to the infallible inerrancy of Scripture with a tenacity extending possibly even to mechanical inspiration in some cases. Rudelbach says that at no point in this period was there greater agreement than concerning inspiration.[31] Bromiley believes that although these early fathers did not teach mechanical inspiration, they did open the way to it by conceiving of inspiration as extending to detailed phrases and by using the term *dictation*.[32] Vawter, however, remarks that "among the early Fathers at least Justin and Athenagoras seemed to have shared a definitely mantic concept of prophecy. Only once in his writings does Justin advert to the personality of an individual prophet."[33]

The same author lists Justin later among those who taught "mechanical dictation," adding, "These were also undoubtedly the views of Theophilus, Clement of Alexandria and Ambrose, of

Athenagoras and Tertullian."[34] It is easy to see that wherever a true dictation theory appears, it carries inerrancy with it. We can (and almost always do) have inerrancy without dictation but never dictation without inerrancy.

AUGUSTINE

Augustine is probably the most important Christian theologian since Paul. His stance toward the Bible was one of his most important theological positions. Consequently a correct understanding of his view is especially important historically.

Augustine's words "I believe in order to understand" have been quoted by Rogers, as well as others, to suggest the purest fideism. I do not think this is a correct interpretation of his meaning. To clarify matters, let us spell out the Augustinian way to knowledge. First, Augustine began with the understanding and not with faith. John E. Smith, whom Rogers cites, acknowledges this: "There are two citations in Augustine's works which speak of the primacy of reason. In these Augustine was presupposing man's capacity for thought."[35] Second, Augustine did not abandon this approach when he came to God. Smith thinks otherwise: "But there are no passages in Augustine's writing where he puts reason before faith as a method of knowing God."[36]

Here we must pause. If Smith's statement means that reason did not precede faith as a method of knowing the existence of God (which is what it suggests), it is palpably false. There is no meaning in saying that Augustine believed in a God of whose existence he had no knowledge, and, of course, Augustine never said such a thing. If it does not mean this, Smith must qualify his statement that Augustine never puts reason before faith as a method of knowing God. But suppose Smith's statement means that reason did not precede faith as a method of knowing in the sense only of experiencing God or savingly knowing God. Smith does not qualify it thus; but even if he did, the statement would still be incorrect. For, according to Augustine, one must first have some knowledge of God if this knowledge is ever to become saving or experiential knowledge. One may have knowledge without faith, but he cannot have faith without knowledge. He cannot experience as God something or someone of which he knows nothing. If Smith's statement may be understood to mean merely that knowledge does not necessarily lead to faith and saving knowledge, it is true. But in this case the interpretation is imprecise, confused, and almost certainly misleading in the context.

But the statement is true in this sense, which is also our third point: Augustine did not abandon the reason/faith approach even as the method of knowing God savingly, though the sequence depended on special divine grace bestowing faith in the context of understanding. This applies especially to the knowing of God in his Word.[37]

Fourth, Augustine's path to saving knowledge is not circular but cyclical. He does not believe in order to understand and in the same sense understand in order to believe. That would be circular and vicious, going nowhere. Rather, first, Augustine understands God, the Word of God, and the reason both are to be believed; second, the gift of faith is bestowed according to the sovereignty of divine grace; and, third, with that faith he understands or experiences savingly ("I believe that I may understand").

Possibly the best way to illustrate Augustine's approach is to listen to him explaining it to a layman. Augustine's *Enchiridion* was his closest approach to a tiny *Summa*. It was a handbook for a layman who had requested it. Here is how the great saint begins:

> These [Christian doctrines] are to be defended by reason, which must have its starting-point either in the bodily sense or in the intuitions of the mind. And what we have neither had experience of through our bodily senses, nor have been able to reach through [our] intellect, must undoubtedly be believed on the testimony of those witnesses by whom the Scriptures, *justly called divine*, were written; and who by divine assistance were enabled, either *through [their] bodily sense or intellectual perception*, to see or to foresee the things in question [italics added].[38]

The italics call attention to the fact that Augustine did not accept the Scriptures without the senses and reason, though they originally did not come through *his* senses and *his* reason, not having been revealed to *him* as they were to the writers of Scripture.[39]

By whatever means Augustine comes to the understanding that the Bible is the Word of God, his inerrancy stance is immediate and unwavering. He writes that "no word and no syllable is superfluous" in Scripture. He confesses, "I have learned to pay them [the canonical books] such honor and respect as to believe most firmly that not one of those authors has erred in writing anything at all."[40] The "hands of the Scripture authors wrote what was dictated by the head," he insisted. "No discordancy of any kind was permitted to exist" in Augustine's Bible. As Seeberg writes, "The highest normative and only infallible authority is, for Augustine, the Holy Scriptures."[41]

Admittedly, Augustine himself on occasion makes remarks that, seen out of the context of Augustinian thought, suggest indifference to biblical inerrancy. For example, Polman often fixes on statements such as the following: though the biblical "authors knew the truth about the shape of the heavens, the Spirit of God who spoke by them did not intend to teach men these things in no way profitable for salvation."[42] But we note that in this and other such statements Augustine did not say that the Bible actually erred in any scientific utterance. On the contrary, the biblical authors "knew the truth about the shape of the heavens." All that is maintained by Augustine is what all inerrancy advocates recognize; namely, that the primary purpose of God's Word is not to reveal "how the heavens go but how to go to heaven" (as one writer put it). However, insofar as the Bible does tell us how the heavens go, it, being God's Word, cannot and does not err. Such information is incidental to a greater purpose; but we are not saying, neither is Augustine, that such information is either erroneous or absent from the inspired Word. Augustine never fell into *non sequitur* no. 3.

Rogers's acknowledgment of Augustine's inerrancy doctrine is marred by the following remark:

> Variant readings were not an ultimate problem for Augustine because the truth of Scripture resided ultimately in the thought of the biblical writers and not in their individual words. Augustine commented: "In any man's words the thing we ought narrowly to regard is only the writer's thought which was meant to be expressed, and to which the words ought to be subservient."[43]

Here we have an error supported by a *non sequitur*. The error is in Rogers's statement that Augustine was not concerned about variant readings because it was the thought and not the words that mattered. The truth is that Augustine did not admit variant readings in the sense of discrepant ones, as his famous remark shows: "*Variae sed non contrariae; diversae sed non adversae* [Variations but not contradictions; diversities but not contrarieties]." In other words, variations were not contradictions that required being overcome by the thought mastering the words. The *non sequitur* is in using the quotation of Augustine as proof that the thought and not the words matter *(non sequitur* no. 3). All that is said is that the words are "subservient." The quotation shows that the thought is the aim of the words and that the words are instrumental to the thought, which presumably could not be reached without them. For Augustine, revealed thoughts without words are impossible and words without revealed thoughts are useless. One is the means and the other the end, but neither is dispensable. What Augustine has joined together (inerrant words and inerrant thoughts) Rogers ought not separate.

So Augustine's inerrancy statements, passed over in silence in *Biblical Authority,* are utterly untouched by anything that anyone has attempted to say against them. The great teacher of the universal church stands as the great teacher of the inerrancy of Holy Scripture.

THE MIDDLE AGES

So far as we know, there is no question that the period of the Middle Ages, especially of the greater scholastics, held firmly to the church's inerrancy doctrine. For Pope Leo the Great, the Scriptures were the "words of the Holy Spirit." Gregory the Great, sometimes called the vulgarizer of Augustine, clearly adhered to this doctrine of an inerrant Scripture:

> Mor. praef. I. 1, 2: Let it be faithfully believed that the Holy Spirit is the author of the book. He, therefore, wrote these things who dictated the things to be written. . . . The Scriptures are the words of the Holy Spirit.[44]

Bonaventura argued that the Bible established truth and held to the formal principle of the Reformation: *Sola Scriptura.* The nominalists were no different on this doctrine. Abelard, for all his heresies, never questioned canonical Scripture. William of Ockham surely gave a dress rehearsal for Luther's historic deliverance at Worms when he wrote that we are not to believe "what is neither contained in the Bible nor can be inferred by necessary and manifest consequence."[45] Likewise, Wycliffe called the Bible the Word of God *explicite* and *implicite.*[46]

The only significant difference of opinion concerning the doctrine of Scripture in the Middle Ages is in the *approach* to inerrancy. It is sometimes supposed that a fideism in Augustine was supplanted by a rationalism in Aquinas. But we have already shown that any fideism in Augustine is mythical. It remains only to be shown that any rationalism in Aquinas is equally mythical.

The medieval synthesis or harmonization of reason and faith did not attempt to show that natural reason and supernatural revelation teach the same thing but only that they are not incompatible. True philosophy and true theology do not contradict each other. No crucifixion of the intellect is necessary in order to believe. Aquinas, for example, taught that saving Christian doctrines were learned only from revelation in the Bible. Reason alone can prove that there is a God who can reveal. It can also refute arguments to the contrary as well as show that there is nothing irrational in revelation and that there are reasons for believing revelation (such as miracles and the testimony of the church). These points are also found in Augustine and the early church. (Later nominalism, to be sure, did lose confidence in these arguments without giving up inerrancy as taught by the church. Indeed, it believed in inerrancy because it was taught by the church.)

THE REFORMATION

Nominalism brings us chronologically and logically to Luther and the Reformation. It is possible that had there been no nominalist Ockham, Luther as Reformer would not have emerged. For not only did the Reformer call William of Ockham his "Liebster Meister" and show the effects of Ockham's ethical and eucharistic thinking, but, most important of all, it was the nominalist's separation of reason and faith that enabled Luther to break the bonds of the approved scholastic system of salvation that had held him.

It seems that exegesis brought about Luther's awakening *(Turmerlebnis)*, sometime before 1513. He had studied under nominalists at Erfurt and Wittenberg, but it was the study of the Bible—especially Isaiah 28:21; Ezekiel 33:11; and Romans 1:17—that produced the evangelical insight. Others had acquired evangelical insights and yet had not gone on to reformation. Why did Luther respond as he did? His response appears to be traceable to his almost simultaneous break with orthodox Scholasticism. On Christmas Day, 1514, He preached his last speculative, scholastic sermon. His sermons on the Decalogue, beginning in 1516 and continuing to February 24, 1517, were directed against Scholasticism. In July he preached his first sermon against the Scholastic doctrine of indulgences. On September 14 of the same eventful year (1517) occurred his first disputation, in which he made the shocking statement that instead of Aristotle being necessary for theology, one could only be a theologian when free of Aristotle.[47] So, a month and a half before the posting of the Ninety-Five Theses, which began the Reformation, the Reformer himself had been born of evangelical insight plus a break with the Scholastic synthesis (thanks to Ockham), which otherwise would have constrained him to renounce that insight.

While we grant—in fact, insist—that Luther and the Reformation were launched with a nonrational, fideistic push, they soon sailed under the traditional reason/faith synthesis. In this respect, the German Reformation (having a bad beginning followed by a good course) is not unlike the English Reformation, which began with Henry VIII's lust but soon went on under its true colors.

In spite of Luther's 1517 denunciation of Aristotle and some subsequent denunciations in the same vein, the Reformer's basic position clearly came to be a harmonization of faith and reason rather than a disharmony. First, concerning Aristotle himself, Luther acknowledged the Greek's value for politics, rhetoric, and the like. Second, we have noticed that Luther's real objection to Aristotle the philosopher was his *guilt by association* with the Scholastic system of grace to which Luther was intransigently opposed. Third, Luther's chief lieutenant, Philipp Melanchthon, used theistic proofs in his *Loci Communes* from the first edition (1521). It is inconceivable that Melanchthon could or would have done this without Luther's tacit approval at least. Fourth and most important is Luther's own profound rationality even where he appears to have exhibited what Ritschl has called an *"irrationalistische Weltanschauung"* (an irrational philosophy or world view).[48]

Rogers observes that Luther said, "For Isaiah vii makes reason subject to faith, when it says: 'Except ye believe, ye shall not have understanding or reason.' It does not say, 'Except you have reason ye shall not believe,'" and "in spiritual matters, human reasoning certainly is not in order."[49] But the latter part of this quotation of Luther explains the former. Once we know that the Bible is the Word of God, then in the "spiritual matters" of which it speaks "human reasoning certainly is not in order." Luther's thought is the same cyclical pattern that we have seen in Augustine and not the vicious circles attributed to him. He does not believe the Bible to be the Word of God without evidence and then accept the evidence because he already believes the Bible. Rather, he first finds reasons for faith in the Bible as the Word of God and then, believing the Bible to be the Word of God, he (reasonably enough) will trust it and not reason thereafter, as seen at Worms.

Again, we say that whatever disagreement there may be concerning Luther's approach to the Bible this, in any case, does not change his view of the Bible's inerrancy. Bodamer has cited hundreds of indubitable utterances of Luther to that effect.[50]

If repetition could establish a position, Luther's would never have been questioned. Why, then, does Brunner, like many others, deny it?[51] Once again, virtually the only reason Luther's inerrancy doctrine is ever questioned is that one *non sequitur* or another is used. Kooiman's favorite is the docetic *non sequitur*, no. 5. He *assumes* that Luther's regarding the Bible as vital precludes verbal inspiration, which is *supposed to be* static.[52] Bromiley's suggestion that Luther departed from tradition because he appreciated the human in the writers is the same *non sequitur* (no. 5).[53] The most commonly advanced argument, too constant to need citation, that Luther denied the canonicity of James and some other parts of the Bible and therefore did not believe in inerrancy is the critical *non sequitur*, no. 4.

More things could be said about Luther's view of an inerrant Scripture, but many of these will appear in our fuller discussion of Calvin's views. With a quotation from Karl Barth we will let the matter rest:

> In the Reformation doctrine of inspiration the following points must be decisive.
>
> I. The Reformers took over unquestioningly and unreservedly the statement on the inspiration, and indeed the verbal inspiration, of the Bible, as it is explicitly and implicitly contained in those Pauline passages which we have taken as our basis, even including the formula that God is the author of the Bible, and occasionally making use of the idea of a dictation through the Biblical writers. How could it be otherwise? Not with less but with greater and more radical seriousness they wanted to proclaim the subjection of the church to the Bible as the Word of God and its authority as such. . . . Luther is not inconsistent when we hear him thundering polemically at the end of his life: "Therefore, we either believe roundly and wholly and utterly, or we believe nothing: the Holy Ghost doth not let Himself be severed or parted, that He should let one part be taught or believed truly and the other part falsely. . . . For it is the fashion of all heretics that they begin first with a single article, but they must then all be denied and altogether, like a ring which is of no further value when it has a break or cut, or a bell

which when it is cracked in one place will not ring any more and is quite useless" *(Kurzes Bekenntnis vom heiligen Sakrament* 1544 W. A. 54, 158, 28). Therefore Calvin is not guilty of any disloyalty to the Reformation tendency when he says of Holy Scripture that its authority is recognised only when it . . . is realised that *autorem eius esse Deum.* In Calvin's sermon on 2 Tim. 3:16 f. (C. R. 54, 238 f.) God is constantly described as the *autheur* of Holy Scripture and in his commentary on the same passage we seem to hear a perfect echo of the voice of the Early Church. . . . In spite of the use of these concepts neither a mantico-mechanical nor a docetic conception of biblical inspiration is in the actual sphere of Calvin's thinking.[54]

CALVIN

Brunner did not see the inerrancy doctrine in Luther but saw it at least in Calvin.

Calvin is already moving away from Luther towards the doctrine of Verbal Inspiration. His *doctrine* of the Bible is entirely the traditional, formally authoritative view. The writings of the Apostles *"pro dei oraculis habenda sunt* [are oracles which have been received from God]" *(Institutio,* IV, 8, 9). Therefore we must accept *"quidquid in sacris scripturis traditum est sine exceptione* [whatever is delivered in the Scripture without exception]" (I, 18, 4). The belief *"auctorem eius (sc: scripturae) esse deum* [God is the author of all Scripture] precedes all doctrine (I, 7, 4). That again is the old view.[55]

While Calvin's traditional verbal inspiration view is generally recognized, the way he is supposed to ground that authority runs something like this:

1. The Holy Spirit's testimony in the soul proves the Bible to be the inspired Word of God.
2. The elect soul accepts the Bible on that basis alone.
3. Nevertheless, there are objective evidences that prove nothing apart from the Holy Spirit. When he proves the Bible by this "testimony," the evidence can be considered confirmatory.[56]

The way this argument is constructed adds nothing to Calvin's fame, but his own line of thought makes sense. First of all, Calvin never conceived of the Holy Spirit as proving inspiration but rather *persuading* of it. His favorite term was *acquiesce.* The Holy Spirit leads the minds of the elect to "acquiesce" in the inspiration of the Bible, the proof of which is in and connected with the Bible data. Calvin was aware that the Holy Spirit does not testify to something of which the person has no idea and for which he has no evidence. He assumed with common sense that men first know the Bible and its claims to inspiration. However, the unregenerate heart, being hostile, needs to be changed by the divine Spirit. The testimony and evidence of the Bible's inspiration is not uncompelling in itself but is stubbornly resisted because of the wickedness of men. The Holy Spirit's role is not to change the evidence (from unsatisfactory to satisfactory) but to change the attitudes of men from resistance to truth to submission to it.

Reason has to precede faith in the sense that the mind has to know what the Bible claims to be. The idea that faith can exist where there is nothing on which it terminates is absurd. There must always be some reason for faith; but so long as the heart will not admit it or acquiesce in it, faith does not follow. In such cases men are inexcusable.[57] The problem is not in the *evidence* but in the *disposition*, and that is what the Holy Spirit deals with. Calvin does not teach that the Spirit *is* the evidence for the inspiration of the Bible. All that he does is lead people to *believe* the evidence.

Calvin's saying that the Holy Spirit's presence is intuited as one intuits the taste of sweetness is not meant as a substitute for argument. The Holy Spirit causes the elect to taste the Bible as the Word of God and "know" (in the sense of experience) that it is divine. When that happens, all stubborn opposition to the rational evidence of the Word disappears. The opposition was artificial to begin with (men "would not" rather than "could not" believe), and this encounter with the Spirit is the existential end of the syllogism sinners had stubbornly been trying to deny. They, like the devil, knew the Bible was the Word of God, but they would not admit it and therefore did not "savingly know" it. Now all that is changed, not because the Holy Spirit has by-passed argument but rather because he has removed the roadblock to it.

An evidence of the insincerity, as well as the noncogency, of contemporary interpretations of Calvin concerns his *indicia* of biblical inspiration. Chapter VIII, Book One of the *Institutes,* reads: "So Far as Human Reason Goes, Sufficiently Firm Proofs Are at Hand to Establish the Credibility of Scripture."[58] The contents of the chapter carry out that label repristinating the classic arguments—past and present—for inspiration. For example, on fulfilled prophecy we read as the title of section 8:

"God has confirmed the prophetic words."[59]

In addition to fulfilled prophecy, all the other stock-in-trade-proofs are unembarrassedly present in Calvin. The insincerity of many modern interpreters comes in here. So far as we know, not one of the neo-Calvinists believes any of these *indicia*. Calvin believed them all, ardently. Acting as if they did agree with Calvin's approach, the neo-Calvinists actually depart from it entirely. Wrongly thinking that Calvin's "confirmations" are nonarguments resting for their validity on the testimony of the Holy Spirit, they confidently agree with their own misconception. Thus, those who slay the prophets academically continue to call them "father." They would not be found dead with those arguments (even as *confirmations*) for which Calvin would have died.

The following citation from Rogers is a good illustration of the way Calvin's modern friends depart from the Reformer while seeming to follow him. "According to Calvin, 'human testimonies,' which are meant to *confirm* Scripture's authority, 'will not be vain if they follow that chief and highest testimony,' as secondary aids to our feebleness. . . . 'Those who wish to prove to infidels that Scripture is the Word of God are acting foolishly for only by faith can this be known.'"[60] These testimonies of men, of which Calvin writes, do confirm the Holy Spirit's testimony; but, how, unless they prove? *If they do not prove, they do not confirm.* If they do prove, then there *is* evidence apart from the Holy Spirit. If there is no evidence apart from the Spirit's testimony, how do these *indicia* confirm? Calvin must, therefore, believe that they do prove, as Rogers *apparently* does not so believe.

But, we ask, if Calvin believes that the testimonies or arguments of men prove the Bible to be the Word of God, why does he say in the following statement that "those who wish to prove to infidels that Scripture is the Word of God are acting foolishly for only by faith can this be known"?

He says this because he means by "prove," not "demonstrate," but "persuade." According to Calvin, these *indicia* demonstrate but they do not and cannot prove (in the sense of persuade) because wicked men suffer not so much from stupidity as from stubbornness. What therefore is needed is a new heart or "faith," which is the gift of God. For an apologist to wish to "prove" to (persuade) infidels (those without faith and having no disposition to believe) that Scripture is the Word of God is to act "foolishly" indeed. For many modern interpreters of Calvin the proof of inspiration cannot be known apart from the Holy Spirit because for them there is no proof of it. By contrast, Calvin presented arguments that any intelligent man could easily know, though he never could "savingly know" or believe apart from the working of God's Spirit.

It is simply not true that Calvin "rejected the rationalistic Scholasticism . . . which demanded proofs prior to faith in Scripture."[61] As we have seen, Calvin did have proofs for Scripture just as the Scholastics did—indeed, the same ones derived through the Scholastics. The "faith" that the Holy Spirit wrought was in these proofs or *indicia*, such as prophecy. For Calvin the Holy Spirit did not work in a vacuum but in the context of Scripture where these proofs were spread out. To be sure, Calvin does not express himself in the Q.E.D. fashion (as in mathematical proofs) of the Scholastics, but his reasoning is the same. Aquinas believed in the testimony of the Spirit, and Calvin believed in the *indicia* of Scripture. Rogers seems to see only their difference in form and not their sameness in substance.

Most modern interpreters of Calvin are the very "spiritualistic sectarians" of whom he complained in his own day—those who claimed revelation from the Spirit apart from the Word. Calvin's Spirit led to the Scripture with its *indicia;* the "spirit" of the modern Niesels, Brunners, and Rogerses is apart from Calvin's Scripture with its proofs of its own inspiration.

Calvin's handling of certain New Testament citations of the Old Testament poses a real problem with reference to Calvin's inerrancy doctrine. In this area Calvin troubled even John Murray.[62] Sufficient to remember here is that Calvin believed in the inerrant inspiration of the New Testament as well as the Old Testament. Consequently, he could easily grant that the Holy Spirit could substitute another word than the original, one that could better express his purpose in the new context. Uninspired men would have no such liberty, though they might *argue* that a new word expresses the meaning for the new context better than the old word that was inerrant. Unless the original word was inerrant, we uninspired interpreters would not be able to fix the original meaning with certainty and consequently could not estimate the most suitable term for explaining it to a new generation. To illustrate, Greenwich Mean Time must be fixed and "inerrant" if we are to express and evaluate our time in a way most suitable for our situation. To illustrate historically, we believe that at the end of the fourth century *homoiousios* ("of like nature") meant essentially the same thing as *homoousios* ("of same nature") at the beginning of the fourth century in the Christological controversies. We are *probably* right, but we *may* be wrong. But, if the Holy Spirit said this he would, of course, be infallibly correct.

As for Calvin's view of inerrancy in relation to matters of science, the issue is much clearer. He maintains that the biblical writers simply wrote in popular style, and popular style does not need to be and indeed cannot be harmonized with science. Popular style is one thing; technical style is another. In an illustration from Calvin, to which Rogers calls our attention, Moses called the moon one of two great lights when in fact it is much smaller than Saturn, as was known even in Calvin's day. There is no problem of harmonization however. As Calvin says, Moses is talking about things as they *appear* to the naked eye; the astronomer, about things as they *are* in the telescope (cf. *non sequitur* no. 1). If the astronomer said that Saturn *appeared* to be bigger than the moon, he would be in error. If Moses had said that the moon *is* larger than Saturn, he would have been in error. But Moses is not in error; and Calvin is not implying error in Moses, though Rogers suggests that Calvin was acknowledging scientific error in Moses and was indifferent to it.[63]

Adding it up, we must say that nothing that modern opponents of inerrancy have presented, cited, deduced, or inferred in any way whatsoever shows that Calvin held any other view than the absolute inerrancy of Holy Scripture. Brunner[64] and Dowey[65] find verbal inspiration in Calvin. Bromiley even finds dictation.[66] Kenneth Kantzer's doctoral thesis may be the most thorough demonstration of Calvin's teaching on inerrancy,[67] and John Murray[68] and J.I. Packer[69] are with him, though they find problems.

POST-REFORMATION SCHOLASTICISM

A.A. Hodge has written somewhere that the seventeenth century with its Scholasticism was the golden age of Protestantism.[70] What Hodge felt to be a natural development and fruition of the Reformation, many today consider a distortion and rigidifying. They see a difference of kind rather than degree, a degeneration rather than shift of emphasis.[71] The difference amounts, however, simply to the Scholastics being more academic, pedantic, and methodical. In a word, the Scholastics were more scholastic.

Therefore, to say of the Lutheran Scholastic, John Gerhard,

that his "doctrine of Scripture . . . was not an article of faith, but the *principium* (foundation) of other articles of faith" and that he therein differed from his mentor, Luther,[72] is unjustified. We have shown that Luther had some reason for faith in the Bible as God's Word, as also did Calvin. Once the Bible was recognized as the Word of God, it, of course, became the *principium* for all truth that it revealed. What else? Even those who hold to partial inspiration believe that the inspired part (if they could identify it) is the Word of God and is to be believed.

Rogers says of the great Reformed Scholastic, Francis Turretin: "Because reasonable proofs must precede faith, Turretin felt it necessary to harmonize every apparent inconsistency in the biblical text. He refused to admit that the sacred writers could slip in memory or err in the smallest matters."[73] Rogers seems to think that Turretin first harmonized every "apparent inconsistency" before he could have faith in the Bible as the Word of God. But he cites no evidence of this, and we are certain that he can find none. Why, then, does he think this? Apparently because Turretin really did refuse to admit any biblical errors "in the smallest matters." If this is the line of reasoning, it is an example of further *non sequiturs:*

1. Turretin admitted no errors in the Bible.
2. Inconsistencies would involve error.
3. Therefore, Turretin:
    a. would admit no inconsistency in the Bible,
    b. would harmonize all apparent inconsistencies, and
    c. would not believe the Bible was the Word of God until he had completed the harmonizations.

It is 3b and 3c that are the *non sequiturs* Rogers apparently does not notice. It does not follow (and it did not follow for Turretin) that because a person believes there are no errors or inconsistencies in the Bible he can harmonize all apparent ones. It is enough that he can show that apparent inconsistencies are not incapable of harmonization. Obviously, if a person does not have to harmonize every apparent inconsistency even *after* believing the Bible to be the Word of God, he does not have to do so *before* believing it.

The jibe of Dill Allison that although Turretin "claimed to be expounding Reformed theology, he never quoted Calvin"[74] is mind-boggling to anyone who knows Turretin's constant allusion to and saturation with John Calvin, whom he admired almost to the point of idolatry.

THE WESTMINSTER CONFESSION OF FAITH

The Westminster Confession of Faith is Presbyterianism's most influential creed. Chapter I, "Of the Holy Scripture," is its most influential and noble chapter. Inerrancy is its indubitable teaching, although the word itself is not used but only equivalents.[75]

The most extensive and scholarly study ever made of this Confession is undoubtedly Jack Rogers's massive, erudite, able, and influential study, *Scripture and the Westminster Confession*.[76] Only his persistent misunderstanding of the faith/reason and total/partial inspiration themes vitiates its value. Because of that volume's significance, Rogers's comments on Westminster in *Biblical Authority* are especially important.

Rogers begins with the fideistic interpretation of the Confession characteristic of his major work:

> Philosophically, the Westminster divines remained in the Augustinian tradition of faith leading to understanding. Samuel Rutherford stated the position: "The believer is the most reasonable man in the world, he who doth all by faith, doth all by the light of sound reason."[77]

Here Rogers cites one of the Westminster divines least disposed to his own thesis, quoting a statement from Rutherford that refutes rather than supports it. If the reader ponders the above quotation, he can see that it boomerangs against the one who cited it. It is meant to show that the Scots' divine, Rutherford, operated on the faith-before-reason principle, but it reveals the opposite. Rutherford calls the believer "reasonable." In other words, there are reasons for faith, for to act by faith is to act reasonably: "he who doth all by faith, doth all by the light of sound reason." Gillespie, another of the "eleven" primary drafters of the Westminster Confession, could not have said it better. This is a utilization and not a crucifixion of reason. There are reasons for faith. That is no crucifixion of the intellect that extols reasonable faith. Rogers continues:

> The "works of creation and providence" reinforce in persons that knowledge which has been suppressed and because of which a person is inexcusable for his sin. Thus there is no "natural theology" in the Thomistic fashion, asserting that persons can know God by reason based on sense experience prior to God's revelation.[78]

Here the point of "reinforce" is missed, just as "confirmation" was in the Calvin discussion. How can creation and providence "reinforce" the innate knowledge of God unless they too reveal God? And what is this but "natural theology," whether exactly the same as Aquinas's or not?

Leaving natural theology and turning to biblical revelation, we read: "The authority of Scripture in section iv was not made dependent on the testimony of any person or church, but on God, the author of Scripture."[79] True, but what Protestant or Roman Catholic Scholastic ever said that the authority of Scripture was "dependent on the testimony of any person or church"? Everyone recognizes that the authority of the Bible rests only on its being God's Word. The testimony of the church or any other proofs are cited only to try to prove that the Bible is the Word of God. If it is the Word of God, its authority is intrinsic. The debate is finished. No "Aristotelian Scholasticism" would try to demonstrate by external evidence the "Bible's authority." All it would try to demonstrate is the Bible's inspiration; and if it succeeded in that, the authority of the Bible would be established *ipso facto.*

Of course, Reynolds, whom Rogers cites, would say—be he Platonist, Aristotelian, Protestant, Roman Catholic, or Jew— that faith is assent "grounded upon the authority of authentical- ness of a Narrator . . ." if that Narrator is believed to be God. Men recognize that in their natural state. The point is only that they do not "see" it spiritually. Reynolds explained this very well in his essay on "The Sinfulness of Sin": "A man, in divine truths, [may] be spiritually ignorant, even where in some respect he may be said to know. For the Scriptures pronounce men ignorant of those things which they see and know."[80] Reynolds is here arguing with the Socinians who deny "spiritual" knowledge altogether in bibli- cal matters. He would now have to argue with Rogers, who denies "natural" knowledge altogether in the same matters.

We continue:

> Section v climaxed the development of the first half of the chapter with the statement that, while many arguments for the truth and authority of Holy Scripture can be adduced, only the witness of the Holy Spirit in a person's heart can persuade that person that Scripture is the Word of God.[81]

This is the statement by which Rogers refutes Rogers on his most fundamental thesis, namely, that faith precedes reason in the historic doctrine of the church and that of Westminster. True to Westminster, he writes, "While many arguments for the truth and authority of Holy Scripture can be adduced, only the witness of the Holy Spirit in a person's heart can persuade." That is, there are arguments of reason that precede faith, though they do not "persuade." This is the view of Origen, Augustine, Aquinas, Luther, Calvin, Turretin, Edwards, and Princeton, but it is not Rogers's faith-before-rationality. The rational is *first;* then, *if the Spirit wills,* comes saving knowledge.

Rogers notes that the last five sections of the Confession delineate the "saving content of Scripture," "the whole counsel of God concerning all things necessary for His own glory, man's salvation, faith and life." Then follows this *non sequitur* (no. 3): "Scripture was not an encyclopedia of answers to every sort of question for the divines."[82] The *non sequitur* (because the Bible is concerned primarily with salvation it is not concerned with other details) is meant to avoid the inevitable inerrancy doctrine. The "saving *content*" is supposed to be one thing, the saving *context* another thing. But they are inseparably woven together in Scripture! No Westminster divine questioned this, and Jack Rogers does not logically deny it. So it does not follow from the fact that the Bible reveals the counsel of God for our faith and life that it does not include answers to incidental questions.

Rogers returns to Rutherford, saying that according to Rutherford, Scripture was not to "communicate information on science. He listed areas in which Scripture is *not* our rule, e.g., 'not in things of Art and Science, as to speak Latine, to demonstrate conclusions of Astronomie.'"[83] True, for Rutherford (as for all other Inerrantists) the Bible is not a textbook of Latin grammar or astronomy, but Rutherford never granted any error of the Bible in science or said that any textbook on science could correctly maintain that Scripture ever erred. Rogers continues with a statement from Rutherford that illustrates *our* point excellently:

> Samuel Rutherford, in a tract against the Roman Catholics, asked: "How do we know that Scripture is the Word of God?" If ever there was a place where one might expect a divine to use the Roman Catholic's own style of rational arguments as later Scholastic Protestants did, it was here. Rutherford instead appealed to the Spirit of Christ speaking in Scripture: "Sheep are docile creatures, Ioh 10.27. *My sheep heare my voyce, I know them and they follow me* . . . so the instinct of Grace knoweth the voyce of the Beloved amongst many voyces, Cant. 2.8, and this discerning power is in the Subject."[84]

When the question is raised, "How do we know that Scripture is the Word of God?" the word *know* is clearly used in the sense of "savingly know." This is evident from Rutherford's answer, which shows that the believer knows Christ's voice savingly by an "instinct of Grace." No *mere* rational knowledge is meant, and therefore no mere rational arguments that Rutherford shared with the Roman Catholics are given. He is not speaking of a knowledge that is "abundantly evidenced" by the many arguments but of a persuasion that comes only from the Holy Spirit. If ever there was a place one might expect a divine to use the Roman Catholic's style of mere rational arguments, it was *not* here.

In conclusion, we read:

> For the Westminster divines the final judge in controversies of religions was not just the bare word of Scripture, interpreted by human logic, but the Spirit of Christ leading us in Scripture to its central saving witness to him.[85]

For the Westminster divines the final judge in controversies was the bare Word of God interpreted by human logic, but the Holy Spirit surely assisted the devout interpreter and spoke in the Word he had inspired. Nevertheless, the divines never appealed to something the Spirit was supposedly saying apart from sound exegesis of his Word. They never attacked an exegesis as not coming from the Spirit but as not coming from the text. As Rogers has noted, these men were not mystics. They did not appeal to any mystical Word but only to the written Word. And they applied their exegesis to *all* questions of religion, such as church government, and not merely to "its central saving witness" to Christ.

In a word, Westminster is saying, What God has joined together—Word and Spirit—let no man put asunder. It is the Spirit who enables the saint savingly to understand the Word, and it is the Word that enables him to understand that it is the Spirit who is enabling him.

AMERICAN THEOLOGY

Before coming to the inerrancy position of old Princeton, we may note that Princeton had no monopoly on this view. Inerrancy was essentially the American position before as well as after old Princeton. We will take but one example prior to the Princeton development—that of America's most distinguished theologian, Jonathan Edwards (d. 1758).

Surprise is sometimes expressed that the Westminster Confession of Faith, chapter I, "Of the Holy Scripture," does not mention directly the argument for inspiration from miracles. We say "directly" because the phrase "incomparable excellencies that do abundantly evidence the Bible to be the Word of God" amounts to an argument from miracles, for how do these things show the Bible to be the Word of *God* except that they affirm God as the miraculous author behind the men he inspired? Nevertheless, miracles are not mentioned explicitly, and that does surprise some.[86] It is interesting, therefore, to find that Edwards, who does expressly make much of the argument from miraculous attestation,[87] subordinates it nonetheless to the "internal" evidence.

In his unpublished sermon on Exodus 9:12-16,[88] Edwards preached that "God gives men good evidence of the truth of his word." This evidence is internal ("evident stamp") especially, but external also. In fact, "there is as much in the gospel to show that it is no work of men, as there is in the sun in the firmament."[89]

This internal evidence appears to include many matters. Edwards approaches the Bible in the context of human need, arguing as follows: First, it is evident that all men have offended God; second, they are sure from providence that God is friendly and placable; third, God is not willing to be reconciled without being willing to reveal terms; fourth, if willing, he must have revealed terms; and, fifth, if the Bible does not have this revelation, the revelation does not exist.[90] After all, there are only three groups of mankind: 1) those who receive the Bible; 2) the Muslims (who derive from it); and 3) the heathen, whose gods are idols and who are judged by the light of nature and philosophy.[91] What insights the heathen do have come from tradition.[92]

Perhaps nowhere has Edwards stated his view of the internal perfections of Scripture better than in the early *Miscellany* 338:

> The Scriptures are evidence of their own divine authority as a human being is evident by the motions, behaviour and speech of a body of a human form and contexture, or that the body is animated by a rational mind. For we know no otherwise than by the consistency, harmony and concurrence of the train of actions and sounds, and their agreement to all that we can suppose to be a rational mind. . . . So there is that wondrous universal harmony and consent and concurrence in the aim and drift, such as universal appearance of a wonderful, glorious design, such stamps everywhere of exalted and divine wisdom, majesty, and holiness in

matter, manner, contexture and aim, that the evidence is the same that the Scriptures are the word and work of a divine mind; to one that is thoroughly acquainted with them, as 'tis that the words and actions of an understanding man are from a rational mind, to one that is of a long time been his familiar acquaintance.

An infant, he continues, does not understand that this "rational mind" is behind a man because it does not understand the symptoms. "So 'tis with men that are so little acquainted with the Scriptures, as infants with the actions of human bodies. [They] cannot see any evidence of a divine mind as the origin of it, because they have not comprehension enough to apprehend the harmony, wisdom, etc."[93] Putting the whole matter succinctly, Edwards says that the Bible shines bright with the amiable simplicity of truth.

As for his argument from miracles as attestation of the biblical revelation, we will confine ourselves to just one miracle: the Jews. "The Jewish nation have, from their very beginning been a remarkable standing evidence of the truth of revealed religion."[94] An earlier *Miscellany* had shown proof that the Jewish religion was divine because of Jewish pride, which could never have accounted for their exalted religion but would rather have worked against it.[95]

That Scripture was inerrant for Jonathan Edwards no one who has ever read his works, especially his sermons, can doubt. *"All* Scripture says to us is certainly true." He adds, "There you hear Christ speaking."[96]

Liberals find this baffling in Edwards but indisputably his opinion:

> George Gordon has written, "It is not edifying to see Edwards, in the full movement of speculation, suddenly pause, begin a new section of his essay, and lug into his argument proof texts from every corner of the Bible to cover the incompleteness of his rational procedure." Peter Gay has very recently written that Edwards was in a biblical "cage." . . . Perry Miller, more than any other student of the Enlightenment, has admired the intellectuality of Jonathan Edwards. Miller sensed that in many ways Edward was not only abreast of our times but ahead of them; nevertheless, he felt Edwards was reactionary in some respects even to his own age.[97]

Still more recently John E. Smith has written:

> The central problem is this: Edwards, on the one hand, accepted totally the tradition established by the Reformers with respect to

the absolute primacy and authority of the Bible, and he could approach the biblical writings with that conviction of their inerrancy and literal truth which one usually associates with Protestant fundamentalism.[98]

PRINCETON THEOLOGY

After an interesting survey of the development of Princeton theology from Archibald Alexander to B.B. Warfield in which Rogers sees it interpreting Westminster in terms of Turretin, incorporating the Aristotelian Common Sense philosophy, and increasingly rigidifying its own position to the point of the inerrancy of the autographa (all of this highly debatable—and worthy of debate if we had space), Rogers observes, "Since the original texts were not available, Warfield seemed to have an unassailable apologetic stance."[99]

First of all, since no evangelical scholar ever defended an infallible translation, where can the written Word of God be located but in the original texts or autographs? This was always assumed. Warfield was no innovator. It is true that some believed the text was transmitted "pure," but in that case we would *have* the autographa. There is no question in any case but that the autographs alone were the written Word of God. Warfield would be amused to be given credit for discovering the obvious.

Second, Warfield believed that we virtually did have the autographa in the form of a highly reliable text.[100] He did not consider himself, therefore, "unassailable." One modern teacher refers to the appeal to autographa as "weasel words," an accusation that surely is as unfair as it is scurrilous. Did the Westminster divines suppose that the Word of God located anywhere other than in the autographa? Where is the "rigidifying"?

But to continue:

> Influenced by this principle [the reliability of sense perception], Hodge showed no trace of the theory of accommodation held by Origen, Chrysostom, Augustine, and Calvin, to explain that we do not know God as he is but only his saving mercy adapted to our understanding. For Hodge: "We are certain, therefore, that our ideas of God, founded on the testimony of his Word, correspond to what He really is, and constitute true knowledge."[101]

We have already shown that Rogers' interpretation of accommodation in the above-named fathers is misleading and erroneous (*non sequitur* no. 2). Hodge is not really differing from the fathers.

After enumerating a dozen Bible verses teaching the immutability of God, Hodge remarks about the phenomenological character of God's repentance: "Those passages of Scripture in which God is said to repent, are to be interpreted on the same principle as those in which He is said to ride upon the wings of the wind, or walk through the earth."[102] God is accommodating himself by using phenomenological language. Hodge also taught the incomprehensibility of God as clearly as Calvin or any other father of the church.[103]

A Continuing Reformed Tradition

Mention is made by Rogers of James Orr, Abraham Kuyper, Herman Bavinck, and G.C. Berkouwer as respected evangelicals who either did not postulate inerrancy or made a fideistic approach to the Bible in the nineteenth and twentieth centuries. We will not challenge this. Many other names could be added, and other centuries as well, but the names of Origen, Augustine, Aquinas, Luther, Calvin, the Westminster divines, Edwards, and the Princetonians, along with the general tradition of the church from the beginning, must be enrolled under the banner of inerrancy.

Inerrancy has almost always been maintained along with biblical criticism. Criticism was never rejected by Hodge, Warfield, Lindsell, or any other scholarly inerrancy advocate of whom we have ever heard. These men and others have tried and found wanting many of the claims of many of the biblical critics, but that they rejected "biblical criticism" as such is unsupported by evidence. Warfield was noted as a New Testament critic as was his famous successor, J.G. Machen. A.T. Robertson was champion extraordinary of the historico-grammatical method. When charges are made to the contrary, it is usually because the *science* of biblical criticism is being confused with the *negativism* of some biblical critics.

Turning now to Berkouwer's concept of biblical errancy, we read:

> Berkouwer commented that when error in the sense of incorrectness is used on the same level as error in the biblical sense of sin and deception we are quite far removed from the serious manner in which error is dealt with in Scripture.[104]

Here Berkouwer seems to allow that the Bible may contain errors in the sense of "incorrectness" since these errors are not on a "level" with such errors as "sin and deception." This can only mean that if the Bible is the Word of God, then God can be incorrect, can err, can make mistakes, though he cannot deceive. This does more than "damage reverence for Scripture." This damages reverence for God.

We realize that these are serious charges—but they are not unwarranted. However, they do not imply that those guilty are deliberately so. We believe they are not and that if they ever see validity in our charge, they will, as the earnest Christians they are, eschew their error in charging God in his Word with error.

Loretz in *Das Ende der Inspirations Theologie* entitles chapter 20 *"Die Wahrheit der Bibel—das theologische Pseudoproblem der absoluten Irrtumslosigkeit der Heilige Schrift"* (The Truth of the Bible—The Theological Pseudo Problem of the Absolute Inerrancy of the Holy Scriptures). He calls inerrancy a pseudoproblem and thus disposes of it as a nonissue. Why is it a false problem or nonproblem? Because the Bible is Semitic, and the concept of inerrancy is Greek: the Bible is affectional, inerrancy is rational; the Bible is nonlogical, inerrancy is logical. It is a case of apples and oranges, according to Loretz. Inerrancy simply asks the wrong questions and gets irrelevant answers. This is Rogers's theme with different names: *Semitic* for Platonic-Augustinian-Reformation-Berkouwer; *Greek* for Aristotelian-Thomistic-Scholastic-Warfield. But, of course, the Jews could think and the Greeks could feel, and the only thing "pseudo" in this whole matter is calling inerrancy a "pseudoproblem."

CONCLUSION

We come now to the bottom line. What does the history of the church show to be her doctrine concerning Holy Scripture? The only inerrant answer I can perceive is inerrancy. That is not to say that every teacher in the history of the church has confirmed or expressly stated the doctrine, but it does maintain that the evidence shows that the overwhelming general consensus of the church and the teaching of her greatest theologians in all branches of her communion has been inerrancy.

Virtually the only reason this has ever been questioned as a historical datum is not in the teachings of the fathers but in the wrong deductions that are sometimes drawn from them, as we pointed out at the beginning of this essay and have illustrated throughout—the persistent *non sequitur*.

Rogers's conclusions after his survey are quite different:

First, it is historically irresponsible to claim that for two thousand years Christians have believed that the authority of the Bible entails a modern concept of inerrancy in scientific and historical details.[105]

Except for the inappropriate word *modern*, the above statement would be correct if the word "not" were inserted between "have" and "believed." There is nothing especially modern in the concept "without error." Rogers apparently believes that associating the concept with scientific matters began in the seventeenth century. But whatever new ideas about science may have appeared then, the concept of accuracy in scientific and historical detail was not among them. Therefore, for Rogers to say that the statement that for two thousand years Christians have believed in the inerrancy of all Scripture is "irresponsible" is irresponsible. It is not Lindsell, cited in the footnote, but Rogers who is irresponsible. Not only have Christians believed this, but most official Christian declarations of the last two millennia have affirmed it. Certainly nothing was ever officially declared to the contrary by an orthodox church.

To make his thesis appear more palatable, Rogers resorts to caricature again, suggesting that the inerrancy view entailed the notion of "some kind of direct, unmediated speech of God, like the Koran or The Book of Mormon."[106] The charge is worse than that of mechanical inspiration, which is the usual erroneous charge urged at this point against inerrancy. Rogers has inerrancy advocates teaching *no* human participation—not even mechanical.

The second conclusion of Rogers is of special interest to the present writer:

It is equally irresponsible to claim that the old Princeton theology of Alexander, Hodge, and Warfield is the only legitimate evangelical, or Reformed, theological tradition in America.[107]

When I first read this statement I agreed with it heartily (and I still do). But I did not at first reading see the footnote that accused me of making that "irresponsible" claim. When someone called the note to my attention, my respect for Rogers is such that I said perhaps I had been guilty by some slip of the pen or unconscious inference. I knew only that I have never believed or intended to teach that the old Princeton position (which is indeed my own) was the "only *legitimate* evangelical, or Reformed, theological tradition in America."

Then I reread my article in *The Evangelicals*[108] to see if I had (unintentionally and mistakenly) given such an impression. I am still reading these pages to find what Rogers had in mind. Could this be another *non sequitur?* Because I teach that the Old Princeton position of inerrancy is the only *sound* tradition, do I therefore teach that it is the only "legitimate" one? I have never contended that any view of Scripture other than inerrancy has been and is illegitimate in my own Reformed denomination or any other evangelical or Reformed denomination unless it so stipulates. None to my knowledge does, with the possible exception of some of the evangelical Lutheran bodies.

Rogers's third conclusion is the most frightening of all, for it would perpetuate the same sins against the future history of the church that have been committed against the past:

> It is no doubt possible to define the meaning of biblical inerrancy according to the Bible's saving purpose and taking [*sic*] into account the human forms through which God condescended to reveal himself. Inerrancy thus defined could be heartily affirmed by those in the Augustinian tradition. However, the word *inerrancy* has been so identified with the Aristotelian notions of accuracy imposed on it by the old Princeton theology that to redefine it in American culture would be a major task.[109]

Being interpreted, this paragraph means that it would be possible, though difficult, to define inerrancy in a new sense to mean errancy in the old sense. This is the extension of an olive branch that turns into a snake when picked up. Let inerrancy continue to mean "without error." Plato would not have any more difficulty understanding that than Aristotle.

If Rogers and many with him do not believe the Bible is without error, let them continue plainly to say so and argue their case. But may God deliver us from evangelicals who follow the liberal practice of "flying at a low level of visibility." Evangelicals are already beginning to speak of errant inerrancy. But let this position not be confused with the historic consensus of inerrancy meaning "without error," PERIOD.

Notes

[1] The title of the volume edited by Jack Rogers (Waco: Word, 1977).

[2] Cf. Markus Barth, *Conversations with the Bible* (New York: Holt, Rinehart and Winston, 1964).

[3] William H. Harris and Judith S. Levey, eds., *The New Columbia Encyclopedia* (New York and London: Columbia University Press, 1975).

[4] Ibid., p. 291.

[5] A.H. Strong asks, "Would it be preferable, in the O.T., if we should read: 'When the revolution of the earth upon its axis caused the rays of the solar luminary to impinge horizontally upon the retina, Isaac went out to meditate' (Gen. 24:63)?" (*Systematic Theology* [Philadelphia: Griffith and Rowland, 1907], 1:223). The great inerrantist Martin Luther was himself committing this *non sequitur* when he condemned Copernicus's heliocentrism.

[6] Arthur Lindsley, "The Principle of Accommodation," an unpublished Pittsburgh Theological Seminary paper (1975), gives a sound current discussion and critique of this *non sequitur*.

[7] George MacDonald carried this *non sequitur* to its logical conclusion when he wrote, "It is Jesus who is the revelation of God, not the Bible." Cited by William B. Glover in *Evangelical Nonconformists and Higher Criticism in the Nineteenth Century* (London: Independent, 1954), p. 82.

[8] Emil Brunner illustrates this *non sequitur* when discussing John Calvin in *Revelation and Reason: The Christian Doctrine of Faith and Knowledge*, trans. Olive Wyon (Philadelphia: Westminster, 1946), p. 275.

[9] This has been a persistent *non sequitur* in neoorthodoxy generally, and Karl Barth has specialized in it (cf. *Church Dogmatics*, vol. I, *The Doctrine of the Word of God*, second half-volume, ed. G. W. Bromiley and T. F. Torrance [Edinburgh: T. & T. Clark, 1956], pp. 523ff.). Klaas Runia has astutely criticized Barth in *Karl Barth's Doctrine of Holy Scripture* (Grand Rapids: Eerdmans, 1962) in an *ad hominem* manner by observing that Barth himself believed that Jesus Christ was true man, without his humanity preventing his sinlessness. Burtchaell has well remarked that God can do what man cannot do: control men without destroying their humanity. "The wrangle over predestination and free will still runs on, for example, because disputants cannot see that God can do what no man can: control the activity of persons without infringing upon their freedom" (*Catholic Theories of Biblical Inspiration Since 1810* [Cambridge: Cambridge University Press, 1969], p. 290).

[10] The history of the doctrine of inspiration has been repeatedly and thoroughly researched. In addition to extensive studies in encyclopedias and histories of doctrine, innumerable monographs have appeared on the subject in general as well as on details such as "alleged discrepancies" (cf. John Haley, *An Examination of the Alleged Discrepancies of the Bible* [Nashville: Goodpasture, 1951]) and individual theologians (cf. A.D.R. Polman, *The Word of God According to St. Augustine* [Grand Rapids: Eerdmans, 1961]). It is sufficient here to note a few of the more important general historical works. Classical nineteenth-century studies include: William Lee, *The Inspiration of Holy Scripture* (New York: Robert Carter and Brothers, 1858); George T. Ladd, *The Doctrine of Sacred Scripture: A Critical, Historical and Dogmatic Inquiry*, 2 vols. (New York: Scribner, 1883). More recently there are William Sanday, *Inspiration: Eight Lecutres on the Early History and Origin of the Doctrine of Biblical Inspiration* (London: Longmans, 1903); G.D. Barry, *The Inspiration and Authority of the Holy Scripture: A Study of the Literature of the First Five Centuries* (New York: Macmillan, 1919); Daniel J. Theron, *Evidence of Tradition* (Grand Rapids: Baker, 1958); Johannes Beumer, *Die Inspiration der Heiligen Schrift* (Freiburg, Basel, and Vienna: Herder, 1968); Bruce Vawter, *Biblical Inspiration* (Philadelphia: Westminster; London: Hutchinson, 1972); Robert M. Grant, *A Short History of the Interpretation of the Bible*, rev. ed. (New York, London: Macmillan, 1972); Daniel Loretz, *Das Ende der Inspirations Theologie: Chancen eines Neubeginns*, 2 vols. (Stuttgart: Katholisches Bibelwerk, 1974).

Just before this volume went to the printer a copy of Stephen T. Davis, *The Debate about the Bible* (Philadelphia: Westminster, 1977) came into my hands. Though not a historical study, it is a most acute analysis of the contemporary debate. While attacking inerrancy and defending a so-called infallibilist position, it is one of the most judicious, balanced, fair critiques I have ever read. Davis avoids virtually all *non sequiturs*, argues to the point, honors motives, recognizes differences, all the while unambiguously affirming orthodox doctrines himself. He admirably embodies the concept of a "worthy opponent." Nevertheless, I believe his argument against inerrancy and for "infallibilism" fails utterly. His attack is unsuccessful because he admits that he cannot prove that "errors" actually do exist in the Bible (cf. chapter 5, p. 14ff.), and this leaves him with only one feeble argument; namely, that the Bible does not explicitly use the word *inerrant* in its self-description. But if it calls itself God's Word many times, thus indicating the inspiration not only of the writers but of the writings as well, what can a divine Word be but an inerrant Word? The mountain is laboring and not even bringing forth a mouse. Davis's own infallibilist position self-destructs, for he admits that his Bible may even err on any crucial doctrine (though he hopes not and thinks it will not), and he admits that ultimate reliance for truth is on his own mind, Scripure notwithstanding (p. 70). Over two hundred years ago, Jonathan Edwards demolished this very argument found in the Deist Matthew Tindal's *Christianity As Old As Creation (Miscellany* 1340 in H. Townsend, *The Philosophy of Jonathan Edwards* [Eugene: University of Oregon Press, 1955]) so thoroughly that I doubt that, if Davis had read that critique, his *Debate about the Bible* would ever have been written.

[11]But Augustine was familiar with Aristotle's logic, which he clearly followed (cf. D. D. Runes, ed. *The Dictionary of Philosophy* [New York: Philosophical Library, 1942], p. 23).

[12]McClintock and Strong, *Cyclopedia of Biblical, Theological and Ecclesiastical Literature* (New York: Harper, 1892), 1:315ff.

[13]*Clement* I, chap. 8, 16, 45.

[14]N. Stonehouse, *The Infallible Word: A Symposium* (Philadelphia: Presbyterian Guardian, 1946), pp. 127, 128.

[15]*Apologetic* I, chap XXXVI.

[16]*Plea for Christians*, IX.

[17]*Autolycus* II, X. Cf. also III, XII. Prophets and gospel writers are said to be "inspired by one Spirit of God."

[18]*Admonition to the Greeks*, XIII.

[19]Eusebius, *Church History*, V, 17.

[20]*Against the Heresies*, III, 16, 2.

[21]*De Opere et Eleemosynis*, chap. 9.

[22]*Apologetic* 18, 20.

[23]*Homily* on Numbers 27:1.

[24]On Matthew 15:14.

[25]Jack B. Rogers, "The Church Doctrine of Biblical Inspiration," *Biblical Authority*, p. 19.

[26]Ibid., p. 20.

[27]Cf. the preface to Chrysostom's *Homilies on the Gospel According to St. John.* He writes, "Seeing then it is no longer the fisherman the son of Zebedee, but He who knoweth 'the deep things of God' (1 Cor. ii. 10), the Holy Spirit I mean, that striketh this lyre, let us hearken accordingly. For he will say nothing to us as a man, but what he saith, he will say from the depths of the Spirit . . ." *(A Select Library of the Nicene and Post-Nicene Fathers of the Christian Chruch*, vol. XIV, p. 2).

[28]Vawter, *Biblical Inspiration*, p. 27.

[29]Ibid, p. 38. Athanasius also may be cited as affirming that inspiration extended to everything in Scripture: "These are fountains of salvation, that they who thirst may be satisfied with the living words they contain. In these alone is proclaimed the doctrine of godliness. Let no man add to these, neither let him take ought from these" *(A Select Library of the Nicene and Post-Nicene Fathers of the Christian Church*, vol. IV, p. 552).

[30]Jerome writes of the Scriptures that they were written "at the inspiration or urging or

even dictation of the Holy Spirit; they were even written and published by him" (Denzinger, *Enchiridion Symbolorum*, pp. 3650ff.).

[31]Ladd, *Doctrine of Sacred Scripture*, vol. 2, p. 154.

[32]Geoffrey W. Bromiley, "The Church Doctrine of Inspiration" in *Revelation and the Bible*, ed. Carl F. H. Henry (Grand Rapids: Baker, 1958), pp. 207-8.

[33]Vawter, *Biblical Inspiration*, p. 14.

[34]Ibid., p. 25.

[35]John E. Smith, *The Analogy of Experience* (New York: Harper, 1973), p. 8. Cited in *Biblical Authority*, p. 21.

[36]Ibid, pp. 9-10. We do not mean to imply that if Augustine had begun by assuming the inspiration of Scripture, this would have affected his inerrancy stance. All present-day presuppositionalists with whom I am familiar do begin by assuming inspiration and most vigorously defend inerrancy. Cornelius Van Til is an outstanding example. Cf. Greg Bahnsen's "Inductivism, Inerrancy, and Presuppositionalism," *Journal of the Evangelical Theological Society*, vol. 20, no. 4 (December 1977), pp. 289-305.

[37]This is the emphasis of Augustine's anti-Pelagian works. Grace as necessary to faith is central.

[38]Augustine, *The Enchiridion*, ed. with Introduction by Henry Paolucci (Chicago: Regnery, 1961), p. 4. The following statement, therefore, seems quite gratuitous: "When applied to theology, the Platonic method assumed that faith preceded and provided a framework to make possible right reasoning."

[39]For those who would explore this theme further we recommend B.B. Warfield, *Studies in Tertullian and Augustine* (New York: Oxford University Press, 1930).

[40]*Epistle* 82, I, 3.

[41]Reinhold Seeburg, *Text-book of the History of Doctrines*, trans. Charles E. Hay (Grand Rapids: Baker, 1966), vol. 1, p. 358, note 1. He cites: *The Doctrines of Christianity*, II, 8; *Epistle* 82, I, 3; *On the Unity of the Church*, 3.5; 13.33; 11.28; *On Baptism*, II, 3, 4; *The City of God*, XI, 3; and *The Enchiridion*, I, 4. C. T. Costello *(St. Augustine's Doctrine of the Inspiration and Canonicity of Scripture* [Washington, D.C.: Catholic University of America, 1930], pp. 30, 31) also argues that Augustine believed in inerrancy.

[42]Cited from Polman, *Word of God*, pp. 59, 60.

[43]Rogers, "Church Doctrine of Biblical Inspiration," p. 21.

[44]Seeberg, *Textbook*, vol. 2, p. 18, note 5.

[45]For a discussion of the *Sola Scriptura* principle, see the essay by R.C. Sproul in this volume—chapter 4: *"Sola Scriptura:* Crucial to Evangelicalism."

[46]*Dialogues*, 411.

[47]*"Error est dicere: sine Aristotele non fit theologus; immo theologus no fit, nisi id fiat sine Aristotele."*

[48]What is said of the ultimate Luther is still more evident of the other great Reformers. No one questions this concerning Ulrich Zwingli, the most humanistic of all. We believe that scholars would never have doubted it in John Calvin either, were it not for erroneous deductions from his doctrine of the internal testimony of the Holy Spirit. The Genevan maintains that there is no true or saving knowledge of God except for those enlightened by the Word and Spirit *(Institutes of the Christian Religion*, ed. John T. McNeill, trans. Ford Lewis Battles [Philadelphia: Westminster, 1960], book I, chap. 7). All knowledge apart from that, however true, is vain. But it is a sad error to attribute to Calvin a denial of any and all knowledge of God apart from the testimony of the Spirit. Men "know" God by the seed of religion in each, by the creation and government of the world, and so forth (ibid., book I, chap. 1, 4). Calvin follows the traditional path even to citing classic Cicero.

[49]Rogers, "Church Doctrine of Biblical Inspiration," p. 24.

[50]W. Bodamer, "Luthers Stellung zur Lehre von der Verbalinspiration," *Theologische Quartalschrift*, 1936, pp. 240ff.

[51]Brunner, *Revelation and Reason*, pp. 275-76.

[52]Willem Jan Kooiman, *Luther and the Bible*, trans. John Schmidt (Philadelphia: Muhlenberg, 1961), *passim*.

[53]Bromiley, "Church Doctrine of Inspiration."

[54]Barth, *Doctrine of the Word of God*, part 2, p. 520.

[55]Emil Brunner, *The Christian Doctrine of God*, trans. Olive Wyon (Philadelphia: Westminster, 1950), p. 111. He also admits that Calvin, as Luther, thought that scholars could compute on the basis of biblical genealogies *(Revelation and Reason*, p. 278, note 13).

[56]This kind of thinking leads Grant to remark that "by his acceptance of the primacy of faith in exegesis Calvin opened the way for subjectivism even while he tried to exclude it" *(Short History of Interpretation*, p. 134), and even Brunner thought Calvin was too subjective *(Revelation and Reason*, p. 269). Admittedly, Calvin's phraseology at times suggests subjectivity.

[57]Compare Romans 1:20 where unregenerate men "know" God but do not have faith or worship him. They hold the truth in unrighteousness. Paul says they are "without excuse."

[58]Calvin, *Institutes*, vol. I, p. 81.

[59]Ibid., pp. 87-88.

[60]Rogers, "Church Doctrine of Biblical Inspiration," p. 27.

[61]Ibid.

[62]John Murray, *Calvin on Scripture and Divine Sovereignty* (Grand Rapids: Baker, 1960), p. 12.

[63]Rogers, "Church Doctrine of Biblical Inspiration," pp. 28-29. Cf. Charles W. Shields, *The Trial of Servetus by the Senate of Geneva: A Review of the Official Records and Contemporary Writings* (Philadelphia: MacCalla, 1893), p. 17; C. T. Ohner, *Michael Servetus: His Life and Teachings* (Philadelphia: Lippincott, 1910), p. 49; C. Manzoni, *Umanesimo ad Eresia: M. Serveto* (Napoli: Guida Editori, 1974), p. 30.

[64]Cf. above, note 56.

[65]Edward Dowey, *The Knowledge of God in Calvin's Theology* (New York: Columbia University Press, 1952), p. 100.

[66]Bromiley, "Church Doctrine of Inspiration," p. 210.

[67]This makes Kantzer's assertion of Calvin's inerrancy position in *Inspiration and Interpretation*, ed. John F. Walvoord (Grand Rapids: Eerdmans, 1957), p. 137, all the more impressive.

[68]John Murray, *Calvin on Scripture and Divine Sovereignty* (Grand Rapids: Baker, 1960).

[69]James I. Packer, "Calvin's View of Scripture" in *God's Inerrant Word*, ed. J. W. Montgomery (Minneapolis: Bethany Fellowship, 1974).

[70]To see the thoroughness of Reformed Scholasticism's development of the inerrancy doctrine, cf. Heinrich Heppe, *Reformed Dogmatics*, trans. G.T. Thomson (London: Allen and Unwin, 1950), pp. 12-47. Robert Preus's *Inspiration of Scripture: A Study of the Theology of the 17th-Century Lutheran Dogmaticians* (Edinburgh and London: Oliver and Boyd, 1955) does the same for Lutheran Scholasticism. Seventeenth-century Roman Catholic Scholasticism was also active in this area (cf. Vawter, *Biblical Inspiration*, p. 66, citing Suarez).

[71]This is a common evaluation by neoorthodox theologians such as Barth and Brunner, who see themselves as truer to the Reformation than its immediate successors. But R.M. Grant also unfortunately remarks that "the later Reformation did not follow Luther, however, and it came to insist on traditional principles of Verbal Inspiration and infallibility which had been alien to him" *(Short History*, p. 135). As we have seen, Luther also contended that the words of canonical Scripture were the inerrant words of God, as his successors confirmed. Bromiley, revealing his fideism, takes a middle path, recognizing that the Scholastics represented only a shift of emphasis but feeling that with them "non-biblical rationalism threatens" ("Church Doctrine of Inspiration," p. 213).

[72]Rogers, "Church Doctrine of Biblical Inspiration," p. 30.

[73]Ibid.

[74]Ibid., p. 31. When I read the Allison statement I leafed through a few pages of the middle of an English translation of Turretin's systematic theology I used with students and found at casual glancing a half dozen citations of Calvin, more than half of which were quotations. Furthermore, the statement that the *Helvetic Consensus* of Heidegger and Turretin "announced that textual criticism of the Old Testament would 'bring the foundation of our faith and its inviolable authority into perilous hazard'" (ibid.) is

distressing. Any reader unfamiliar with the *Consensus* would suppose from this statement that it was opposed to biblical criticism as such. If anyone will read the two relevant paragraphs in *Creeds of the Churches,* ed. John Leith (New York: Doubleday, 1963), pp. 310-11, he will see that the concern of the *Consensus* was with mere conjectural emendation by the critics "sometimes from their own reason alone" of the "Hebrew original." One does not have to agree with the critical opinion of *Consensus* to recognize its genuine concern lest the word of man be substituted for the Word of God. I believe in textual criticism myself, but I know textual critics who amend the text at the drop of their critical hat, including sometimes the text of the New Testament, which has no vowel-point problem. I oppose such subjective textual criticism and am therefore (like the *Consensus)* sometimes thought, unfairly, to be opposed to valid textual criticism.

[75]Cf. also chap. XIV: "By this faith a Christian believeth to be true *whatsoever* is revealed in the Word, for the authority of God Himself speaketh therein."

[76]Jack B. Rogers, *Scripture and the Westminster Confession* (Grand Rapids: Eerdmans, 1967).

[77]Rogers, "Church Doctrine of Biblical Inspiration," p. 33.

[78]Ibid.

[79]Ibid.

[80]B. Riveley, ed., *The Whole Works of the Right Rev. Edward Reynolds,* 6 vols. (London: Holdsworth, 1826), 1:103.

[81]Rogers, "Church Doctrine of Biblical Inspiration," pp. 33-34.

[82]Ibid., p. 34. Note the caricature of the inerrantists' view by making it represent the Bible as an "encyclopedia of answers to every sort of question." Caricature usually reveals the threadbare character of one's own case in that it requires a distorted view of the oppstion to survive.

[83]Ibid., p. 34.

[84]Ibid., p. 35.

[85]Ibid.

[86]Cf. E.D. Morris, *Theology of the Westminster Symbols* (Columbus: Champlin 1900).

[87]Dozens of his *Miscellanies* refer to this subject directly and indirectly.

[88]Cited with the kind permission of the Beinecke Library and Rare Book Room, Yale University.

[89]Sermon on Ephesians 3:10 in *The Works of President Edwards* (New York: Carvill, 1830), 7:66ff.

[90]Unpublished sermon outline on 2 Timothy 3:16, points 6 and 7.

[91]Unpublished sermon on Luke 1:77-79.

[92]Jonathan Edwards, *Miscellany* 1337. Cf. 1338.

[93]Ibid.

[94]Edwards, *Miscellany* 1290-91.

[95]Edwards, *Miscellany* 811.

[96]Outline sermon on 2 Timothy 3:16 in Alexander B. Grosart, ed., *Selections from the Unpublished Writings of Jonathan Edwards* (Edinburgh: Ballantyne, 1865).

[97]John H. Gerstner, "An Outline of the Apologetics of Jonathan Edwards," *Bibliotheca Sacra* 133 (July-Sept. 1976): 195.

[98]*Review of Metaphysics* 30 (Dec. 1976): 306.

[99]Rogers, "Church Doctrine and Biblical Inspiration," p. 39.

[100]Cf. John H. Gerstner, "Warfield's Case for Biblical Inerrancy" in *God's Inerrant Word,* pp. 136-37.

[101]Ibid., p. 140.

[102]Charles Hodge, *Systematic Theology* (New York: Scribner, 1873), 1:391.

[103]Ibid., pp. 337-38.

[104]*Biblical Authority,* p. 44.

[105]Ibid.

[106]Ibid., p. 45.

[107]Ibid.

[108]*The Evangelicals,* ed. David F. Wells and John D. Woodbridge (Nashville: Abingdon, 1975), pp. 21-37.

[109]Rogers, "Church Doctrine and Biblical Inspiration," p. 45. But Clark Pinnock is trying, according to Rogers (cf. footnote).

ENCOUNTERING PRESENT-DAY VIEWS OF SCRIPTURE

James I. Packer

James I. Packer is Associate Principal of Trinity College, Bristol, England. He was educated at Oxford University, where he took degrees in classics, philosophy, and theology and secured his doctorate in 1954 for research on the Puritan Richard Baxter. Following two years' service on the staff of a church in Birmingham, he was Senior Tutor of Tyndale Hall, an Anglican Seminary, 1955-61; Warden of Latimer House, a study center in Oxford, 1961-70; and Principal of Tyndale Hall, 1970-71. Following the merger of Tyndale Hall with two other colleges to become Trinity College in 1972, he assumed his present position. Dr. Packer is the author of "Fundamentalism" and the Word of God, Evangelism and the Sovereignty of God, God Speaks to Man, Knowing God, *and* I Want to Be a Christian, *as well as two chapters (*"Sola Scriptura *in History and Today" and* "Calvin's View of Scripture") *in* God's Inerrant Word, *edited by J.W. Montgomery.*

2 *James I. Packer*

ENCOUNTERING PRESENT-DAY VIEWS OF SCRIPTURE

T HREE GENERAL observations will make clear the standpoint from which I write.

THEOLOGY AND RELIGION

First, *when you encounter a present-day view of Holy Scripture, you encounter more than a view of Scripture.* What you meet is a total view of God and the world, that is, a total theology, which is both an ontology, declaring what there is, and an epistemology, stating how we know what there is. This is necessarily so, for a theology is a seamless robe, a circle within which everything links up with everything else through its common grounding in God. Every view of Scripture, in particular, proves on analysis to be bound up with an overall view of God and man. Nowadays, awareness of this fact seems to be fairly general, due to the intense and self-conscious preoccupation with questions of method that has marked theology, along with most other fields of study, during the past half-century. We all now know (don't we?) that your method and presuppositions—in other words, the things you take for granted—will always have a decisive influence on your conclusions. So there should certainly be no difficulty in getting agreement on the point that you do not encounter any view of Holy Scripture, or of any other doctrinal matter, at proper depth till you see it as part of a larger intellectual whole and understand how it relates to and "works" within the unity of that larger unit.

Indeed, to take the full measure of a view of Scripture, you must go wider than that and explore its implications for religion. For each set of theological convictions (of which the view taken of Scripture will form an integral part) belongs to a total view of religion, that is, of right behavior and relationships toward God, as well as of right beliefs and reasonings in one's own mind. No theology can be properly evaluated except in the light of the religion to which it prescribes, explains, and justifies.

Calvin saw this; hence he composed his theological textbook under the title *Institutio Religionis Christianae* (Instruction in Christian Religion), writing into it a treatment of the basic realities of Christian living and making it breathe a spirit of devotion and doxology throughout. Puritans and seventeenth-century continental Reformed theologians saw the point too and hence defined theology in ways that highlighted its practical and religious thrust; thus, Perkins called it "the science of living blessedly for ever,"[1] and Turretin described it as *"theoretico-practica . . .* more practical than speculative."[2] More recently, the Anglican Austin Farrer showed himself aware of the same point when he said somewhere that something must be wrong with Tillich's theology, because it could not be prayed. (Nor can it; Tillich himself later in life made the sad admission that he had given up prayer for meditation.) The evaluative relevance of the practical implications of a position is surely too plain for anyone to deny.

But for all that, the link between theology and religion is something that Protestant theologians today, as for the past hundred years, repeatedly ignore. They talk and write as if they see theology as just an intellectual exercise of forming and analyzing notions; they treat the practical bearing of these notions as someone else's concern rather than theirs; they isolate topics artificially for speculative treatment, thus losing sight of the very nature of theology; and they fail to draw out the wide-range implications of each notion for Christian obedience. The trouble no doubt is that these theologians have been too busy keeping up with the philosophical Joneses in the secularized university circles where so much of their work is done and discussed and have been too little concerned to sustain their churchly identity and role. On this, Eric Mascall speaks the word in season:

> What I hold as essential for the theologian is that his theologizing should be an aspect of his life as a member of the Body of Christ; he

needs to be under not only an academic but also a spiritual ascesis, as indeed all the Church's greatest theologians have been . . . the theologian needs insight and he needs conversion, neither of which are simply the routine application of rules.[3]

Agreed! But meanwhile we have to cope with the effects of a century of failure at this point, and the effects are that, on the one hand, theology has been made to look like an intellectual game divorced from life and, on the other hand, theological notions are not usually evaluated by the test that is most decisive, namely, whether they further or impede the practice of biblical religion. Thus, for example, Clark Pinnock, in his helpful chapter in *Biblical Authority*, "Three Views of the Bible in Contemporary Theology," observes the convention and lacks the element of practical and religious evaluation that his avowed concern for spiritual renewal might have been thought to require.[4] In this essay I try to write pastorally and practically, as a would-be church theologian, rather than in the manner of a secularized academic.

EVANGELICALISM AND SCRIPTURE

Second, *when you encounter the evangelical view of Holy Scripture, you are encountering the source, criterion, and control of all evangelical theology and religion.* Chillingworth's open-textured dictum that the Bible alone is the religion of Protestants can mean several things, not all of them acceptable, but it fits evangelicalism most precisely. Methodologically, evangelical theology stands apart from other positions by its insistence on the clarity and sufficiency of the canonical Scriptures, and evangelical religion is distinctive by reason of the theology and the method of application that determines it. Let me spell this out.

Roman Catholicism, Anglo-Catholicism, and Orthodoxy characteristically say that though the God-given Scriptures are a sufficient guide for faith and practice in themselves, they are at key points unclear and can rightly be understood only by the light of the church's God-taught tradition. By contrast, Protestantism's many blends of rationalism, mysticism, and existentialism (unstable compounds, all of them) characteristically say that while it is fairly clear what beliefs and behavior patterns the Bible writers want their readers to adopt, the books vary so much from each other, and Scripture as a whole stands at such a distance from the modern world, that the Bible cannot be a sufficient guide for today till what it says is sieved, edited, and recast in the light of all that our age takes for granted. Let it be said that both positions invoke the Holy Spirit, the former as author of both Scripture and tradition, the latter as illuminating mind and conscience to enable each individual to formulate his personal understanding of Christianity. Let it also be said that both types of position are held with learning and integrity and admit of a great deal of internal debate and adjustment (a factor that tends to prolong the life of scholarly options), and there is no sign of their imminent decease. Not, of course, that their vitality implies that either is wholly right.

Against both, evangelicalism characteristically says that Scripture is both clear and sufficient; that the God-given Scriptures are the self-interpreting, self-contained rule of Christian faith and life in every age; that, though the canonical books were composed over a period of more than a thousand years, during which significant cultural shifts become apparent in the records themselves, they do in fact present within the framework of progressive declaration and fulfillment of God's saving purpose in Christ a consistent view of how God deals with men; that, since God does not change nor, deep down, does man, this view remains true, timely, and final; and that the central covenanted ministry of the Holy Spirit is to lead us to the Scriptures that he inspired, to open the Scriptures to us, and so to induce both conceptual and relational knowledge of the Father and the Son to whom the Scriptures introduce us. It is further characteristic of evangelicalism to insist that both the church and the individual Christian must live by the Bible (that is, by appropriate contemporary application of biblical principles); that the proper task of the teaching and preaching office that God has set in the church is to explain and apply the Scriptures; and that all beliefs, disbeliefs, hopes, fears, prayers, praises, and actions of churches and Christians must be controlled, checked, and where necessary reshaped—*reformed*, to use the good old word—in the light of what God is heard saying as the Spirit brings biblical principles to bear.

Evangelicals see this methodology as entailed in acknowledging the divine authority of the teaching of Christ's apostles, whose message we have firsthand in the New Testament letters, and of their Lord, to whose mind, as all sober criticism allows, the Gospels give ample access. For the teaching of Christ and the apostles includes, on the one hand, a use of Old Testament Scripture, taken in conjunction with their own message, which assumes that God's definitive instruction comes in both, and, on the other hand, a diagnosis of the fallen and unaided human mind as dark, perverse, insensitive, incapable, and untrustworthy in spiritual matters, needing to be enlightened and taught by God at every point. Though all men have an inescapable awareness of God that comes by way of his creation (Rom. 1:19-21, 28, 32), there can be no natural theology of traditional Thomist type: only through Scripture are these inklings of our Maker brought into true focus, by being integrated with the revelation of the living God that Scripture contains.[5] Scripture here means the Old Testament that Christ and his apostles attest, plus the New Testament, which their own inspiration produced, and for true knowledge of the true God we are shut up to Scripture absolutely. So, at any rate, evangelicals see the matter.

Scripture shows us Jesus Christ, and it is happily true that Christians of many schools of thought—Roman Catholic, Orthodox, neoorthodox and "liberal evangelical" Protestants, and charismatics of all sorts—speak from time to time of the ministry of the Christ who is Savior, Lord, and God and of communion with him through the Spirit, just as evangelicals do. Sometimes it is urged that those who speak so should be seen as all evangelicals together, sharing a common faith in Christ and proclaiming a common message about him. For the measure of truth in this estimate we should thank God. Yet the deeper and, for our present purposes, the more relevant truth is that the rigorous biblical methodology described above sets the evangelical position apart as something distinctive and unique. My own standpoint in this present essay is that of a would-be consistent evangelical at this deeper level.

THE INERRANCY DEBATE

Third, *when you encounter the current evangelical debate on Holy Scripture, you are encountering an awkwardly confused situation.* What is it all about? Professedly, it is about inerrancy. Men like Harold Lindsell and Francis Schaeffer urge the importance of a clear confession that the Bible is totally trustworthy, not erring in any of its declarations. I believe they are right and have done well to raise their voices. But why is this confession important?

Here the awkwardness of cross purposes and divided values begins to appear. Some predict that once inerrancy as an avowed principle is given up, it is only a matter of time before all the outlines of Christian supernaturalism will be eroded away, as happened in the liberal Presbyterianism of the past half-century, and that institutions and churches that do not insist explicitly on the factual truth of Scripture at all points will soon be unable to maintain a full testimony to the gospel of Christ. Behind this "domino" thinking lies a sense that once any biblical declaration is disbelieved, the evangelical methodology is abandoned, the floodgates of skepticism are opened, and biblical authority as a principle runs aground on the sandbank of subjectivism, where it can be expected to break up completely. Others, however, object that what the domino thinkers mean by inerrancy is a body of (1) interpretations of texts, (2) harmonizations of phenomena, (3) argumentations against older types of skepticism and (4) formulations of the doctrine of Scripture against which the Bible itself sets a question mark; and that the real issue is whether, as a matter of evangelical method, we are free to submit to biblical, historical, and theological analysis the "inerrancy tradition" of the past one hundred years to see if it is really scriptural enough. Whether there is substantial disagreement about the nature and place of Scripture as such—that is, about God and the Bible—as well as about interpretative techniques and preferred ways of speaking in apologetics and dogmatics—that is, about man and the Bible—is so far unclear. Nor is it yet apparent whether the weight of the debate is on how to approach and handle Scripture or on how to define inerrancy and how far it is politic to use this term in Christian communication—whether, that is, the argument is essentially about things or about words.

The dim light of the discussion, allied to the heat that it generates, makes clarity hard to achieve, and debate is never easy when the state of the question is unclear. Also, because of the way in which academic faculties have lined up, it is hard to take any position in the debate without seeming to call into question someone else's competence or good name as an evangelical, and this is most unfortunate. In the present essay, I try to spell out my own position without attempting to adjudicate on that of others.

ENCOUNTERING LIBERAL VIEWS

What Pinnock calls "the curious coalition known as conservative evangelicalism" (why curious? one wishes that he had told us) is, in fact, a transdenominational Protestant family, united by a common faith in Jesus Christ as our sin-bearing Savior and divine Lord and a common purpose of allowing God in Christ to rule our minds and lives through the Bible. With this purpose goes a common understanding of the Bible's basic contents, which the striking unanimity of evangelical systematic theology over four centuries reflects.[6] Also, underlying this body of shared convictions is, as we saw, a common recognition that God himself has taught us the principle of biblical authority through the words of our Lord and of the New Testament writers. Squabbles within the family as to how in detail the principle should be applied presuppose agreement on the need to apply it: the arguments have to do only with establishing a proper technique for the task. Thus we find that the world-wide evangelical constituency today displays an impressive solidarity of conviction and purpose, and with that an impressive and increasing international cohesiveness, of which such a document as the tight-packed Lausanne Covenant, 3,000 words long, produced in a congress lasting just over a week and assented to by some 4,000 Christians representing 151 countries, is striking proof.[7]

The case with liberal Protestantism, however, is quite different.

What is liberal Protestantism? It really is "a curious coalition," for the resemblances that make up the liberal family likeness are more negative than positive. The positive principle that gives liberalism its basic identity is Schleiermacher's view of religion as a sense of God that is caught rather than taught and can be put into words in more than one way. Then a further major element in that identity has been the polemic, more or less explicit, that liberalism has maintained against evangelical belief in revealed truth. Polemics, however, like adversity, can make strange bedfellows; shared peeves do not guarantee common purposes, and liberals are often at each others' throats, much oftener, it would seem, than evangelicals. The word *liberal* is usually explained by those who espouse it as voicing their claim to a spirit of liberality, that is, of tolerance, flexibility, openness to new ideas, and freedom from doctrinaire dogmatism; though whether self-styled liberalism always shows this spirit is a question that, if explored, might leave some faces red. But what convictions do liberals as a body share? Three motifs constantly appear, all with a decidedly negative slant.

First, liberal Protestantism affirms, in Pinnock's words, that "divine truth is not located in an ancient book but in the ongoing work of the Spirit in the community, as discerned by critical rational judgment."[8] Note, however, that "divine truth" means to liberals, not God's instruction nor a permanently valid human formulation, but simply an authentic awareness of God, to which no particular form of words is necessary either as a means or as an expression. As J. Gresham Machen pointed out half a century ago in *Christianity and Liberalism,* the liberal position in all its forms is deeply anti-intellectual in both its stance and its thrust, and this explains why it is so consistently hostile to the attempts of both Roman Catholics and evangelicals to formulate a definitive theology on the basis of a supposedly definitive Bible.

Second, liberal Protestantism espouses a type of Christology that is not "from above" in the sense of seeing Jesus Christ as the divine Son, the second person of the Godhead, and the eternal Word made flesh, according to John's Gospel, Philippians 2, Colossians 1, and Hebrews 1–2, which the Nicene and Chalcedonian formulae follow. Instead, liberal Protestant Christologies are "from below," seeing Jesus in "humanitarian" terms as a prophetic, God-filled man, an archetype of religious insight and excellence, one who, however much he carries for us what Ritschl called the "value" of God, is not God in person. Such Christologies involve, of course, abandoning all thought of a real ontological Trinity and a real divine sin-bearer. They require a reconstructed view of salvation in which Christ's mediation appears as a matter of teaching and trail-blazing only, with no hint of his having borne the Creator's wrath against our sins in order to render him propitious to us—for it would take a divine person to do that. Liberals characteristically cut the knot here by denying that there is any personal wrath of God against us that needs to be quenched and maintain a barrage of criticism against "word-made-flesh" Christology as being necessarily docetic, minimizing the true humanness of our Lord.

It seems right to class all existentialist Protestant positions that build on a "humanitarian" Christology, even those that, like Bultmann's, came out of neoorthodoxy, and that affirm a real "Christ of faith" transcending the "historical Jesus," as jazzed-up liberal Protestantism rather than anything else.

Third, liberalism highlights human religious greatness, as seen in the Bible, in Jesus, and in all Christian, pagan, and secular pioneers who have in any way contributed to man's "humanization" by stressing life's spiritual and moral values. Rightly does Pinnock say that liberals have sought to replace the idea of the

Bible's infallibility as teaching from God with what they saw as "proper respect for its human greatness" as "a classical witness of those in whose lives God once worked which can once again serve to alert us to his reality";[9] but there is need to go further and underline the deep difference between the mystical and moral naturalism of the liberal idea of religious greatness, of God in men's lives, and of the redemptive supernaturalism of those who censure these ideas biblically, in terms of fellowship with God through a divine Savior. A very great gulf is fixed between those who see Jesus' greatness and signifigance for us in his human God-consciousness (so Schleiermacher), or in his ethics (so Ritschl, Harnack, and Albert Schweitzer), or in his self-understanding as a man in God's hands and his example of loyal and hopeful commitment (so Ernst Fuchs, James Robinson, and the authors of the British symposium *The Myth of God Incarnate*)[10] and those who, with the writer to the Hebrews, see his greatness in terms of his being our divine-human high priest who put away sins and now saves to the uttermost (cf. Heb. 10:21; 7:4; 9:25-26). The width of that gulf must be stressed; it can hardly be exaggerated.

The point needing emphasis is that liberal Protestant views of Scripture, as indeed of all else relating to our redemption, differ from the generic conservative evangelical view, not just in detail, but in their whole frame of reference. It is naive and misleading to present the theological relationship between the two types of view (as distinct from the partnership they rightly maintain in the pretheological exercise of historical exegesis) in terms of partial agreement and partial disagreement. The deeper insight was and remains that of Machen, who half a century ago saw here two rival religions that at fundamental level relate to each other only by mutual contradiciton and in polemical grapple. Even the word *God* has radically different meanings in the two systems. Granted, some moderns call themselves liberals without espousing fully characteristic liberal views; granted, liberals use a biblical and evangelical vocabulary (though in a changed and diminished sense); granted, some of today's liberals were yesterday's conservative evangelicals, who see their current views as a natural outgrowth of what they held before. Yet the basic antithesis between the two types of position remains. The Bible that is thought of as man's testament of religious feeling, self-understanding, and ethical inklings is not really the same book as the Bible that is received as God's testimony to himself, even if the sixty-six books with their almost two million words coincide in both cases. The two types of theological interpretation of Scripture do not mesh at all. It would have been helpful if Pinnock had underlined this more clearly.

Encountering Neoorthodox Views

The word *neoorthodox* has always been somewhat loosely used. For half a century it has stood as a label for that body of theological work that, following the lead of Karl Barth, has sought a way back from liberalism to the revelation-shaped, salvation-centered orthodoxy of the Reformation without returning to belief in the inerrant inspiration of the Bible on which that orthodoxy rested. The fact that, though far from unanimous on matters of substance, neoorthodox theologians shared this common purpose justifies Pinnock's reference to neoorthodoxy as "a trend in contemporary theology."[11] "Contemporary," however, coming from an author writing in 1977 is not quite right. It is true that for something like a generation after 1930 the neoorthodox program was a matter of prominent, perhaps dominant concern among Protestant theologians; but by about 1965 interest had clearly moved to the problems of ontology, epistemology, and hermeneutics pinpointed by Bultmann's call to demythologize in order to communicate, and there it remains. Also, while it is true that positions characteristic of neoorthodoxy are still held, the neoorthodox pilgrim trail is empty today, simply because the old liberalism that was its starting point is now a thing of the past. It is from other places in the wilderness that theologians traveling toward the gospel start today.

In the following paragraphs, Karl Barth is the main object of attention. That is because he was not only the first but also in many ways the greatest of neoorthodox teachers; also because, being a "dazzlingly brilliant"[12] writer who gave the world, along with some five hundred other items, the *Church Dogmatics*, an unfinished *summa theologiae* of over seven thousand pages, he is likely to have more long-term influence than other theologians of this type; also because neoorthodoxy appears at its strongest intellectually and its noblest spiritually in the writings of Barth, and his weaknesses, however great, are comparatively less than the corresponding defects of others on the same trail. It should, however, be realized that Barth stands at the extreme right of the

neoorthodox spectrum; that others who shared his overall purpose (Emil Brunner and Reinhold Niebuhr, for instance) did not
backtrack so far from the man-centered liberalism in which they
were reared as Barth did; that some who were with him at the start
in hoisting the banner of God's transcendence with the ropes of
Kierkegaard's existentialism, and were thought of as neoorthodox
in consequence, never got through to anything like Reformation
faith in Christ (Rudolf Bultmann and Friedrich Gogarten, for
instance), so that their views, if thought of as in any sense standard, make Barth's look utterly perverse (and vice versa, of
course); and finally that in Barth's account of Jesus Christ the
Word, the God-man, Creator and Redeemer, presupposition and
determinant of all that is not God and representative of all mankind both as reprobate and as elect, there really are major eccen-
tricities of his own, by which his otherwise impressive teaching is
deeply flawed.[13]

It is to Barth's credit that he laid constant stress on God's
sovereign freedom and lordship in grace, on man's incapacity in
his sin to feel after God and find him, on the reality of God's
communion with us through the Word that he speaks to us in
Christ, and on the instrumentality of the Scriptures in conveying
to us the knowledge of Christ and of grace that they exhibit. It is to
Barth's credit too that the "Procrustean bed" of his theological
method, whereby he collapses all doctrines concerning God and
his creation into Christology, whatever its shortcomings in other
ways, presupposes and builds on a substantially Nicene
Trinitarianism, a Chalcedonian Christology, an acknowledgment
of Jesus' death and resurrection as the work of God saving mankind, and a robust confidence that the biblical witness to Jesus
Christ, which is God's own witness given through man's, can be
truly and precisely expressed in the propositions and theses of
rational, disciplined theological discourse. The irrationalism,
skepticism, arbitrariness, and ultimate incoherence involved in
Emil Brunner's so-called dialectical method, which keeps our
minds perpetually in unstable equilibrium as they fly between
poles of assertion and denial of the same truth, and of belief and
disbelief of biblical teachings,[14] were abandoned by Barth at an
early stage and became more and more conspicuous by their
absence from successive volumes of the *Church Dogmatics*.

Since Barth never repudiated liberal skepticism about the
space-time factuality of some biblically recorded events, choosing

rather to ignore and bypass it, and since he never developed a rational apologetic making ontological and epistemological links between what Scripture tells us and the rest of our knowledge, but derided such ventures as vicious, his teaching is beclouded with mists of ambiguity. Though it seems clear that he meant to define and describe a Christ whose virgin birth, crucifixion, and resurrection were, and whose future return will be, facts of public space-time history, it is an open question whether his exclusively kerygmatic method, allied to his use of phenomenological categories for expressing the contents of revelation, enables him to anchor his Christ in the world of objective reality as well as in that of the theologian's fertile mind.[15] But even if we think that the answer to this question is no, there is much to admire in and learn from Barth's treatment of particular themes.

What does Barth say about the Bible?[16] His basic idea is that the Bible is the means whereby the event of revelation takes place, for in and through its human witness to God, God constantly discloses himself to us. The confession of biblical inspiration (*theopneustia*) concerns in the first instance not its divine origin in the past but its divine instrumentality in the present. This view may reflect a doubtful exegesis of *theopneustos* in 2 Timothy 3:16 and involve something of a false antithesis, but its positive thrust is welcome, and merits our approval. And though, as Pinnock notes, Barth makes quite a meal of rejecting any formal ascription of inerrancy to the Bible and of affirming its "capacity for errors," he declines to identify particular mistakes in it, although he declares in general terms that there are some, both factual and religious.[17] On the contrary, "while preaching the errancy of the Bible, Barth practices its inerrancy":[18] his interpretations, while sometimes novel and unconvincing, are always presented as elucidations of the witness the text actually bears, without any suggestion that anything it says should be discounted as false. Evangelicals will applaud Barth's exegesis as correct in method, if not always in substance; but we must realize that by stating that the prophets and apostles erred in their writings, even if we cannot say where, Barth himself has made his exegetical method seem hazardous, arbitrary, and untrustworthy. There is ruinous irrationality here. As Colin Brown says (twice!), "It is impossible to maintain high doctrines of revelation and inspiration without at the same time being willing to defend in detail the veracity and historicity of the biblical writings."[19] But here Barth fails us, and the effect of his failure is to make it seem unreasonable for anyone, himself included, to trust the texts as he does. Sadly, it must be recorded that other neoorthodox thinkers see this very clearly, and therefore do not so trust them.

The truth is that the neoorthodox enterprise of trying to re-establish the authority of biblical teaching on salvation while rejecting biblical teaching on Scripture is inherently inconsistent and self-contradictory; thus, all versions of neoorthodoxy, like all versions of liberalism before them, exhibit a built-in arbitrariness that it is not possible to eliminate. There is no road to rational faith this way. Barth's exegesis shows him ready in practice to treat the testimony of all texts as divine truth, but his general statement that the human authors made errors in Scripture, even in its religious and theological content, can be squared with his practice only if we suppose that in his view *either* some biblical statements are true in their character as God's Word but erroneous in their character as man's word (which is surely incoherent nonsense, though some who have looked to Barth for inspiration have talked this way), *or*—and this is the way Barth himself seems to lean—the divine message of the passage does not always coincide with the human writer's meaning, since God is free in the event of revelation to use the human words any way he pleases. But that opens the door to allegorizing and turns God's gift of insight into Scripture into the bestowal of uncheckable private revelations. There seems no way out of this dilemma.

Something similar must be said from a methodological stand-point about "biblical theology" as practiced by such teachers as Sir Edwyn Hoskyns, Oscar Cullmann, Gabriel Hebert, Michael Ramsey, and John Bright during the past half-century. Like neoorthodoxy, with which indeed it has conscious links, this movement has sought to reapprehend the faith of the biblical writers, reading the Bible "from within," and, like neoorthodoxy, it has highlighted the character of Scripture as witness to God in history and its instrumentality in communicating God and his Word to human hearts today. The method of identifying with biblical faith is impeccable, but it is inconsistently applied, for biblical faith includes the conviction that Scripture as such, being God's Word (both what he *said* and what he *says*), is wholly true and trustworthy, and "biblical theology" has regularly allowed itself to "criticize the Bible by the Bible," as the procedure has been described; that is, to set up a privately selected "canon within the canon" as a standard for determining what biblical teaching is valid and what is not. It has to be said, however, that nothing in biblical faith itself justifies one's doing this; on the contrary, one who does it parts company, methodologically at least, with biblical faith, and throws doubt on the seriousness of his announced intention always to "be biblical."

Nor is it only exponents of neoorthodoxy and "biblical theology" who lapse in this way. Pinnock detects the same faulty method in Dewey Beegle, who identified himself as an evangelical critic of inerrancy, and in Paul King Jewett, who sets out to correct Paul's supposedly sub-Christian utterances on the relation of the sexes in Christ by his Christian ones. As Pinnock says, the natural implication of this method is that "in Scripture God does not always speak, requiring the reader to determine where he speaks and where he does not. In principle this seems to be liberal . . . theological methodology."[20] As an Englishman who can look back over some seventy years of self-styled "liberal evangelical" British theology, based on just this approach, I can only sigh agreement. The method is arbitrary and false, involving both denial and disruption of the unity of biblical teaching that those who seek find. The method of integrating Scripture with Scripture in interpretation—the method Calvin called the "analogy of Scripture," and the confession of biblical inerrancy safeguards— is the only method with biblical warrant, and the only one that can keep us from the impoverishment to which an unsanctified selectiveness will otherwise lead.

Encountering Roman Catholic Views

One might have expected that on the topic of biblical inerrancy, if on no other, evangelicals would be able to look to Roman Catholics as their natural allies, for during the past century official Roman Catholic assertions of inerrancy have been frequent and explicit. In 1957, in his book *The Authority of Scripture,* J.K.S. Reid began his chapter on "The Roman view" with this statement: "The Roman Church stedfastly adheres to the doctrine of the infallibility and inerrancy of Holy Scripture," followed by a weighty if tortuous quotation from Leo XIII's encyclical *Providentissimus Deus* (1893), as follows:

> All the books which the Church receives as sacred and canonical,
> are written wholly and entirely, with all their parts, at the dictation
> of the Holy Ghost; and so far is it from being possible that any error

can co-exist with inspiration, that inspiration not only is essentially incompatible with error, but excludes and rejects it as absolutely and necessarily as it is impossible that God himself, the Supreme Truth, can utter that which is not true.[21]

Rome has always officially held that Scripture has the nature of, among other things, revealed truth and that inspiration entails inerrancy; the historical cleavage between Rome and the Protestant churches over the Bible concerns its interpretation and authority, not its inspiration.

The strength of Rome's past commitment to inerrancy can be gauged from the fact that when the Modernist Abbé Loisy, in the manner of Protestants like Harnack then and Bultmann since, rejected biblical inerrancy in the course of his fundamental questioning of Jesus' divinity and bodily resurrection and the authenticity of Paul's Christianity, the encyclical of 1907, *Pascendi Gregis*, that preceded his excommunication quoted against him the words of Augustine: "In an authority so high [i.e., Scripture], admit but one officious lie, and there will not remain a single passage of those apparently difficult to practice or to believe, which on the same most pernicious rule may not be explained as a lie uttered by the author willfully to serve a purpose. . . ."[22] The domino thinking of Lindsell and Schaeffer about inerrancy has thus some striking precedents! Rather than risk further challenges to inerrancy, Roman Catholic authorities largely clamped down on critical biblical scholarship from the time of the Loisy affair to Pius XII's 1943 encyclical, *Divino Afflante Spiritu*, and it is only since then that it has really flowered.

But Roman Catholic biblical criticism has tended to develop as a getting in on the skeptical act that has now been a liberal Protestant speciality for a century and a quarter, and Reid anticipated in 1957 that the Roman Catholic Church would have to "choose between a recession of sympathy toward criticism and a diminution of the principle of biblical inerrancy."[23] At the second Vatican Council (1962-65) the choice was clearly if unobtrusively made. The Council affirmed: "Since everything asserted by the inspired authors or sacred writers must be held to be asserted by the Holy Spirit, it follows that the books of Scripture must be acknowledged as teaching firmly, faithfully and without error that truth which God wanted put in the sacred writings for the sake of our salvation."[24] This looks at first sight like a reassertion of the older position without change, but it seems to have

been drafted with a view to its functioning as a hole in the dike of
biblical inerrancy, and that is certainly how Roman Catholic
theologians since Vatican II have used it. Bishop B.C. Butler, for
instance, in his authoritative book *The Theology of Vatican II*,
argues that this statement guarantees as inerrant only truths
necessary to salvation, though Scripture contains a great deal
more material than this, and his position is typical.[25] Hans Küng
has gone so far as to deny that God's saving "truth" has the nature
of divine assertions, that is, revealed truths.[26] Though individual
conservatives still maintain the older view, it does not look as if the
Church of Rome will ever officially go back to it. The dike has
been breached.

The significance of this change should not, however, be exaggerated. After all, the Roman Catholic faithful are required to take
their beliefs from the infallible church, as embodying the true
interpretation of Scripture, rather than directly from a Bible that
they have ventured to interpret for themselves. There is a sense in
which Rome, relying on the infallibility of the church, does not
need biblical inerrancy to undergird anything. But for evangelical
Protestants the issue is more serious—and this brings us to our
last section.

THE CRUCIALITY OF INERRANCY

In the light of what we have seen so far, three matters seem to
call for comment as I close.

First, *what does the confession of biblical inerrancy mean?*

Pinnock is one for whom *inerrancy* is "a strong, excellent term
when properly understood."[27] For him it "declares the conviction
that the Bible is our divine teacher by means of which God himself
meets, instructs, saves and corrects us."[28] But because, as commonly used, the word 1) centers attention on the lost autographs
of Scripture rather than its present life-giving power in whatever
form it meets us; 2) emphasizes "questions of factual detail—
historical, grammatical, cosmological and the like"—rather than
the focal point of Scripture, which is Christ and the truth concerning him; and 3) is not usually qualified clearly enough from a
hermeneutical standpoint to make plain that it refers only to what
each writer meant his readers to gather and learn from what he
wrote,[29] Pinnock will not insist on anyone using it, provided one
does not "settle for an alternative which is really weak and per-
missive, allowing one to side-step the teachings of Scripture."

Pinnock raises a series of questions: Is this notion of inerrancy scriptural? logically entailed by inspiration? capable of clear definition? necessary as a basis for learning from the Bible? a central concept involved in grasping what is central in Scripture? an assertion honestly justifiable in the light of the phenomena of Scripture? a proper criterion of authentic evangelicalism? Believing, it seems, that one who understood the word in what has become the usual way (see above) could responsibly decline to say yes to any of these questions and yet retain a credible evangelical identity, Pinnock invites us to conclude that the inerrancy debate is sterile and profitless and that what we should all be doing is working harder together on the factual and theological interpretation of the biblical text and on the task of theological construction in the light of the Scriptures.[30]

If Pinnock's account of what "inerrancy" has come to mean is taken as the whole truth, his argument might seem to be the last word on its subject; and certainly, I have no quarrel with its positive thrust. But I think there is more to be said. Pinnock has not fully focused the logical function that the word *inerrant*, when applied to the Scriptures, fulfills for evangelicals in defining, circumscribing, and safeguarding correct theological method. Starting where Pinnock starts, namely with a recognition that words mean what they are used to mean, neither more nor less, I venture to affirm that when evangelicals call the Bible "inerrant," part at least of their meaning is this: that in exegesis and exposition of Scripture and in building up our biblical theology from the fruits of our Bible study, we may not 1) deny, disregard, or arbitrarily relativize, anything that the biblical writers teach, nor 2) discount any of the practical implications for worship and service that their teaching carries, nor 3) cut the knot of any problem of Bible harmony, factual or theological, by allowing ourselves to assume that the inspired authors were not necessarily consistent either with themselves or with each other. It is because the word *inerrant* makes these methodological points about handling the Bible, ruling out in advance the use of mental procedures that can only lead to reduced and distorted versions of Christianity, that it is so valuable and, I think, so much valued by those who embrace it.

The second matter requiring comment is: *What does the confession of biblical inerrancy accomplish?*

What has just been said shows the answer. Where this confes-

sion is not made, Scripture will not all be taken with all seriousness, elements of its teaching will inevitably be ignored, and the
result, as Lindsell and Schaeffer with others correctly foresee, is
bound to be a certain diminution of supernatural Christian
faith—as we have seen in the various versions of liberalism,
neoorthodoxy, and "biblical theology" and as we must now expect to see in new forms in tomorrow's Roman Catholicism. But
the confession of inerrancy, though it cannot guarantee sound
exegesis or agreement among scholars on just what this or that
text means, does make a full and faithful articulation of biblical
Christianity possible in principle, whereas apart from this confession it is not possible even in principle.

A warning should perhaps be voiced here against the psychological trap (for it is psychological, a matter of falsely associated
feelings, rather than logical, a formal mistake in inference) of
supposing that the confession of inerrancy involves a commitment
to treat all narrative and predictive passages in Scripture as if they
were written according to the conventions that would apply to
ordinary English prose used today for these purposes, rather than
the conventions of their own age and literary genre. Put thus, the
mistake sounds too silly for anyone to make, but in fact it is made
frequently: hence Pinnock's complaint that not enough care is
taken to attach the necessary hermeneutical qualifications to
inerrancy as an idea. And one can see how the mistake happens:
people feel, sincerely if confusedly, that the only natural,
straightforward way to express their certainty that the contents of
Scripture are contemporary in their application is to treat Scripture as contemporary in its literary form. So, for example, Genesis
1 is read as if it were answering the same questions as today's
scientific textbooks aim to answer, and Genesis 2 and 3 are read as
if they were at every point prosaic eyewitness narratives of what
we would have seen if we had been there, ignoring the reasons for
thinking that in these chapters "real events may be recorded in a
highly symbolic manner,"[31] and books like Daniel, Zechariah,
and Revelation are expounded in total disregard of the imagina-
tive conventions of apocalyptic. But it does not follow that because Scripture records matters of fact, therefore it does so in what
we should call matter-of-fact language.

We have to realize that the confession of inerrancy, like that of
the inspiration that entails it, implies nothing at all about the
literary character of particular passages. The style and sense of

each passage must be determined inductively in each case, by getting to know its language, history, and cultural background and by attending to its own internal characteristics. Some Bible narratives are written in plain, unvarnished, eyewitness prose, and some are not. Which are which? We will find out only as we go and look.

But my point is that though the confession of inerrancy does not help us to make the literary judgments that interpretation involves, it commits us in advance to harmonize and integrate all that we find Scripture teaching, without remainder, and so makes possible a theological grasp of Christianity that is altogether believing and altogether obedient. Without this commitment, no such grasp of Christianity is possible. So, despite its negative form, this disputed word fulfills in evangelical theology a most positive, enriching, and indeed vital function, comparable with that fulfilled by the Chalcedonian negatives concerning the union of our Lord's two natures in his one person ("without confusion, without change, without division, without separation"). In both cases the negative words operate as a methodological barrier-fence that keeps us from straying out of bounds at the behest of unruly rationalistic instincts and digging for the gold of understanding where no gold is to be found.

The third matter requiring comment is: *Why is the confession of inerrancy important?*

Again, the answer is clear from what has already been said. It is important that we should embrace a fully believing method of biblical interpretation and theological construction and it is equally important that the fellowship of evangelical theologians—of all theologians, as far as possible—should be based on a common commitment to such a method. The point is surely plain enough by now, and need not be argued further. And let it be added that this point is a substantial rather than a verbal one. Words are not magic; each man has a right to use them in the way that best expresses what he has in mind. So if with, for instance, G.C. Berkouwer[32] and, as it seems, teachers at Fuller Seminary[33] we think the word *inerrant* tainted through its past associations with literary insensitiveness and an improper rationalism in interpreting Scripture, and so prefer not to use it but to say "infallible" instead, that is our privilege. But what, in that case, our colleagues in evangelical theology have a right to expect from us is a clear demonstration in both word and action that we are nonetheless committed to what, in the light of the foregoing paragraphs, may be called the "inerrancy method." Given this, we shall be able to walk together, whatever words we elect to use—not, however, otherwise.

Notes

[1]Ian Breward, ed., *William Perkins* (Abingdon: Sutton Courtenay, 1970), p. 177.

[2]Francis Turretin, *Institutio Theologiae Elencticae* (Utrecht and Amsterdam, 1701), Locus I, Question VII, 6, 15. See also Gisbert Voetius: "'Practical theology' may mean, in the broad sense, all theology that follows Scripture or is based upon it . . . because all theology among pilgrims on earth is in its nature practical, and no portion of it can be correctly and completely discussed unless it is developed practically; that is, applied to the practice of repentance, faith, hope, and love, or to consolation or exhortation" *(Reformed Dogmatics,* ed. John W. Beardslee III [New York: Oxford University Press, 1965], p. 265).

[3]E.L. Mascall, *Theology and the Gospel of Christ: An Essay in Reorientation* (London: SPCK, 1977), p. 60. Mascall alludes to a remark that he quoted from Bernard Lonergan: "The real menace to unity of faith does not lie either in the many brands of common sense or the many differentiations of human consciousness. It lies in the absence of intellectual or moral or religious conversion" (pp. 54-55).

[4]Clark Pinnock, "Three Views of the Bible in Contemporary Theology," in *Biblical Authority,* ed. Jack Rogers (Waco: 1977), pp. 49-73.

[5]This was the point of Calvin's famous image of the spectacles: "Just as, when you put before old or bleary-eyed and weak-sighted men even the most beautiful book, though they may recognize that there is something written they can hardly make out two words, yet with the aid of spectacles they will begin to read distinctly; so Scripture, gathering up the otherwise confused knowledge of God in our minds, having dispelled our dullness, clearly shows us the true God" *(Institutio Christianae Religionis,* I. vi. 1)).

[6]See J.I. Packer, *God's Inerrant Word,* ed. John Warwick Montgomery (Minneapolis: Bethany Fellowship, 1974), pp. 55ff.

[7]For the text of the Lausanne Covenant, together with the Congress papers and addresses that lay behind it, see *Let the World Hear His Voice,* ed. J.D. Douglas (Minneapolis: World Wide Publications, 1975).

[8]Pinnock, "Three Views of the Bible," p. 53.

[9]Ibid, p. 51.

[10]John Hick, ed., *The Myth of God Incarnate* (London: SCM, 1977; Philadelphia: Westminster, 1978). The contributors are John Hick, Michael Goulder, and Frances Young (Birmingham University); Maurice Wiles, Dennis Nineham, and Leslie Houlden (Oxford University); and Don Cupitt (Cambridge University). The thesis the essays seek to establish is that "Jesus was (as he is presented in Acts 2:21) 'a man approved by God' for a special role within the divine purpose, and that the later conception of him as God incarnate, the second person of the Trinity living a human life, is a mythological or poetic way of expressing his significance for us" (p. ix).

[11]Pinnock, "Three Views of the Bible," p. 54.

[12]Colin Brown, *Karl Barth and the Christian Message* (London and Chicago: Inter-Varsity, 1967), p. 140. Pinnock, "Three Views of the Bible," p. 56, speaks of Barth's "massive brilliance."

[13]For a bird's-eye view of this, see Brown, *Karl Barth,* chapter 4, "Barth's Christ-centered Approach to God, Creation and Reconciliation," pp. 99-139.

[14]The best study of the knots into which Brunner's dialectic ties him is that by Paul King

Jewett, *Emil Brunner's Concept of Revelation* (London: James Clarke, 1954).

[15]Reasons for doubting Barth's success at this point are given by C. Van Til in *Christianity and Barthianism* (Philadelphia: Presbyterian and Reformed, 1962).

[16]See Brown, *Karl Barth,* pp. 35-67, 143-47; Gordon H. Clark, *Karl Barth's Theological Method* (Philadelphia: Presbyterian and Reformed, 1963), pp. 185-225; Klaas Runia, *Karl Barth's Doctrine of Holy Scripture* (Grand Rapids: Eerdmans, 1962); and, from a distinctively Barthian standpoint, J.K.S. Reid, *The Authority of Scripture* (London: Methuen; New York: Harper, 1957), pp. 194-221. Barth's own discussions are in *Church Dogmatics,* I. 1, ch. 1, pp. 51-335 and I. 2, chs. 3 and 4, pp. 457-884 (Edinburgh: T. & T. Clark, 1936, 1956).

[17]"The prophets and apostles as such, even in their office, . . . were . . . actually guilty of error in their spoken and written word" *(Church Dogmatics,* I. 2, pp. 528-29). Scripture's "capacity for error . . . extends to its religious or theological content." Yet "we must be careful not to be betrayed into . . . playing off the one biblical man against the other, into pronouncing that this one or that has 'erred.' From what standpoint can we make any such pronouncement?" (p. 509).

[18]Pinnock, "Three Views of the Bible," p. 57.

[19]Brown, *Karl Barth,* pp. 62, 146.

[20]Pinnock, "Three Views of the Bible," pp. 69-70, referring to Dewey M. Beegle, *Scripture, Tradition, and Infallibility* (Grand Rapids: Eerdmans, 1973) and Paul King Jewett, *Man as Male and Female* (Grand Rapids: Eerdmans, 1975).

[21]Reid, *Authority of Scripture,* p. 103; *Providentissimus Deus,* xxiii, echoing the statements of the Council of Trent (Session IV) in 1546 that Holy Scripture was "dictated either orally by Christ or by the Holy Ghost," and of the First Vatican Council in 1870 that the Scriptures "contain revelation, with no admixture of error," and that "having been written by the inspiration of the Holy Ghost, they have God for their author" *(Constitution on Revelation,* ch. II). For ways in which Roman Catholic theologians have worked out these formulae, see J.T. Burtchaell, *Catholic Theories of Biblical Inspiration since 1810* (Cambridge and New York: Cambridge University Press, 1969).

[22]Cited from David F. Wells, *Revolution in Rome* (Chicago: Inter-Varsity; London: Tyndale, 1973), p. 29.

[23]Reid, *Authority of Scripture,* p. 155.

[24]*Constitution on Revelation,* 11.

[25]Butler, *The Theology of Vatican II* (London: Darton, Longman and Todd, 1967), p. 56. See also John Warwick Montgomery, "The Approach of New Shape Roman Catholicism to Scriptural Inerrancy: A Case Study for Evangelicals," in *Ecumenicity, Evangelicals and Rome* (Grand Rapids: Zondervan, 1969), pp. 73-93.

[26]See *Infallible? An Inquiry* (Garden City, N. Y.: Doubleday, 1971).

[27]Pinnock, "Three Views of the Bible," p. 68.

[28]Clark Pinnock, "The Inerrancy Debate among the Evangelicals," in *Theology, News and Notes* (Fuller Theological Seminary: special issue, 1976), p. 11.

[29]Ibid., p. 12. He goes on to say that when inerrancy is qualified as it should be by reference to the author's purpose in writing, one can "fairly say that the Bible *contains* errors but *teaches* none, [and] that inerrancy refers to the *subjects* rather than all the terms of Scripture [and] to the *teaching* rather than to all the *componenets* utilized in its formulation."

[30]Pinnock, "Three Views of the Bible," pp. 62-70.

[31]James I. Packer, *"Fundamentalism" and the Word of God* (London: Inter-Varsity Press; Grand Rapids: Eerdmans, 1958), p. 99. It must be a private mental extrapolation from this phrase that led Pinnock to suppose that I should not agree with Francis Schaeffer's insistence, in *No Final Conflict* (Downers Grove: InterVarsity Press, 1975), pp. 33-34, that the special creation of Adam, and of Eve from Adam, is part of what Genesis 2 teaches (see Pinnock, "Inerrancy Debate," p. 13, note 8). But a glance at the paragraph from which this phrase comes will show that Pinnock's inference was unwarranted and that his supposition is in fact quite false. His whole footnote is most unfortunate.

[32]See G.C. Berkouwer, *Holy Scripture* (Grand Rapids: Eerdmans, 1975), p. 265.

[33]The Fuller Seminary Statement of Faith declares: "All the books of the Old and New

Testaments, given by divine inspiration, are the written word of God, the only infallible rule of faith and practice. They are to be interpreted according to their context and purpose and in reverent obedience to the Lord who speaks through them in living power" (III). David Hubbard, president of the Seminary, formulates the questions currently in debate as follows: "1) Is inerrancy the best word to use to describe the Bible's infallibility and truthfulness? 2) If inerrancy is to be used, how do we define it in a way that accords with the teaching and the data of Scripture?" ("The Current Tensions: Is There a Way Out?" *Biblical Authority*, p. 178).

THE WITNESS OF THE BIBLE TO ITS OWN INERRANCY

Gleason L. Archer

Gleason L. Archer is Professor of Old Testament, Trinity Evangelical Divinity School, Deerfield, Illinois. He holds degrees from Harvard College, B.A., A.M.; Princeton Theological Seminary, B.D.; Suffolk University Law School, LL.B.; and Harvard Graduate School, Ph.D. Dr. Archer has authored: In the Shadow of the Cross *(a translation of* Jerome's Commentary on Daniel),*commentaries on* The Epistle to the Hebrews *and* The Epistle to the Romans, *and* Survey of Old Testament Introduction. *Before coming to Trinity in 1965, he served as student pastor of two churches in New Jersey, Assistant Pastor of Park Street Church, Boston, Massachusetts, and Professor of Biblical Languages and Acting Dean at Fuller Theological Seminary, Pasadena, California. He has served as president of the New England Association of Christian Schools.*

3 *Gleason L. Archer*

THE WITNESS OF THE BIBLE
TO ITS OWN INERRANCY

DOES THE Bible actually assert its own inerrancy as the revealed Word of God? Does it really lay claim to freedom from error in all that it affirms, whether in matters of theology, history, or science? Are proponents of this view truly justified in their insistence on this high degree of perfection in Scripture, or are they actually going beyond what it affirms concerning its own authority? These questions have been raised by those who advocate a lower concept of biblical authority, and it is important for us to settle them as we seek to come to terms with the Bible's own witness.

Before we launch into an examination of specific passages in Scripture that bear upon this question, it would be well to define as clearly as possible the basic issues involved. Otherwise we may lose sight of the objectives of this type of investigation.

PRELIMINARY CONSIDERATIONS

Inerrancy is attributed only to the original manuscripts of the various books of the Bible; it is not asserted of any specific copies of those books that have been preserved to us. Some early portions of the New Testament have been discovered by archaeology (such as the Rylands Papyrus 457 fragment of John 18, and the Magdalen fragment of Matthew 26), dating from the second century A.D., within a century of the original composition of those Gospels. The earliest complete copy of an Old Testament book is still the Dead Sea Scroll of Isaiah (1QIsa[a]), dating from the mid-second century B.C. There are some Qumran fragments of the Pentateuch that are even earlier, coming from the third or fourth century. All these tend to support the received text of the Hebrew and Greek Scriptures as preserved in the standard scholarly editions (Nestle and Kittel). There is far more textual support for the text of Holy Scripture than there is for any other book handed down to us from ancient times, whether the works of Homer, the Attic tragedians, Plato, Cicero, or Caesar. Nevertheless, these are not the original manuscripts, and minor errors have crept into the text of even these earliest and best copies of the books of the Bible. There are occasional discrepancies in the spelling of names, in the numbers cited in the statistical records, and similar matters. It is the special task of textual criticism to analyze these errors and choose the best of the variant readings according to the standard rules (or "canons") of this science.

Yet there is an important qualification to be made in regard to the range or degree of error that has crept into our received text of Scripture. That is to say, the extent of deviation from the exact wording of the original manuscripts of the Bible must somehow have been kept within definite limits, so as not to pervert the sense or the teaching of the passage in which it occurs. Otherwise it could not serve as a trustworthy record of God's redeeming love for mankind or of his will for our salvation. Since the Bible repeatedly affirms that it sets forth the revealed Word of God ("Thus saith the Lord"), rather than the mere conjectures or traditions of men, it must have been preserved in a sufficiently accurate form to achieve its salvific purpose for the benefit of the human race. God is present in Scripture as the omnipotent Lord of history, and as such he could not have allowed his redemptive plan to be thwarted by a seriously defective transmission.

What confirmation do we have that God has in fact maintained that kind of control over the preservation of the manuscripts? The answer is in the critical apparatus appearing in the scholarly editions of the Old and New Testament. Many hundreds of ancient manuscripts have been carefully consulted in drawing up this apparatus, both in the original languages themselves and in the languages into which they were translated (from the third century B.C. to the fifth century A.D.). Yet a meticulous examination of all the variant readings appearing in the apparatus shows

that no decently attested variant would make the slightest difference in the doctrinal teaching of Scripture if it were substituted for
the wording of the approved text. (By "decently attested variant"
we, of course, exclude all merely conjectural emendations, with
which the apparatus of Kittel's *Biblia Hebraica* is needlessly en-
cumbered. We refer only to deviations indicated by actual Hebrew, Greek, Latin, or Syriac manuscripts as over against the
Masoretic Text of the Hebrew Bible, or the Nestle edition of the
New Testament.)

The same finding can hardly be sustained for any other ancient
document preserved to us in multiple copies, whether the Egyp-
tian *Book of the Dead*, the Behistun Rock inscription of Darius I, or
the Middle Kingdom novel know as *The Tale of Sinuhe*. These all
present differences in wording that affect the actual message or
teaching of the document. Only of the Bible is it true that such a
degree of deviation is not found. How may this be accounted for?
It is best accounted for by the supposition that God the Holy
Spirit has exercised a restraining influence on the preservation of
the original text, keeping it from serious or misleading error of any
kind.

So far as the text of the New Testament is concerned, the
testimony of Frederick Kenyon is quite conclusive:

> Repeated mention of divergent manuscripts and families of texts
> may perhaps give the impression that the text of the New Testa-
> ment is abnormally uncertain. Such an impression can best be
> corrected by an attempt to envisage the early history of the text and
> its present condition. So far from the New Testament text being in
> an abnormally unsatisfactory state, it is far better attested than
> that of any other work of ancient literature. Its problems and
> difficulties arise not from a deficiency of evidence but from an
> excess of it. In the case of no work of Greek or Latin literature do we
> possess manuscripts so plentiful in number or so near the date of
> composition. Apart from Virgil, of whom we have manuscripts
> written some three or four hundred years after the poet's death, the
> normal position with regard to the great works of classical litera-
> ture is that our knowledge of their text depends upon a few (or at
> most a few dozen) manuscripts, of which the earliest may be of the
> ninth or tenth or eleventh century, but most of the fifteenth. In
> these conditions it generally happens that scientific criticism has
> selected one manuscript (usually but not necessarily the oldest) as
> principal authority, and has based our printed texts on this, with
> some assistance from conjecture. . . . In the case of the New Tes-
> tament . . . the vellum manuscripts are far earlier and far more

numerous; the gap between the earliest of them and the date of composition of the books is smaller; and a larger number of papyri have (especially since the discovery of the Chester Beatty papyri) given us better means of bridging that gap. We are far better equipped to observe the early stages of textual history in the manuscript period in the case of the New Testament than of any other work of ancient literature.[1]

THE ORIGINAL MANUSCRIPTS

The question naturally arises in this connection: If we do not now possess the inerrant original manuscripts, what is the point of arguing that they must have been free from all error? Why do we not simply accept the fact that textual errors have crept into the wording of the Bible as we now have it and try to make the best of it in its imperfect form? Is it not enough for us to maintain that even in that form it can present us with an "infallible rule of faith and practice" (to use the standard phrase of the Westminster Confession of Faith)?

In answer to this, it should be pointed out, first of all, that there is a great difference between a document that was corrupted with error at the start and a document that was free from mistake at its original composition. If the original author was confused, mistaken, or deceitful, then there is little to be gained by employing textual critical methods to get back to an approximation of the original form. The errors and misinformation inhere in the archetype itself and serve only to the disadvantage and hurt of the reader. Only if the original was correct and trustworthy is any useful purpose served by elimination of copyists' errors. The pursuit of textual criticism itself implies a trustworthy original, the original wording of which has decisive importance.

Second, it should be observed that the controlling influence of an inerrant model is part of our daily experience today, even though none of us has access to that model. In the Bureau of Standards in Washington, D.C., there is preserved a perfect pound, a perfect foot, a perfect quart—all the basic measures of weight, length, and volume, in relation to which all other pound-weights, rulers, quart bottles, and other measures are judged. Very few Americans have ever seen these standard models in Washington with their own eyes. Yet none would contend that we may completely disregard them on the ground that all we ever see are approximate measuring devices.

Third, if mistakes at any level characterized the original manuscripts of the Bible, the effort to discover in them a truly "infallible rule of faith and practice" becomes an exercise in futility. Most of the doctrinal teaching contained in Holy Scripture comes to us in a framework of history and science. For example, the opening statement of the Apostles' Creed affirms that God the Father Almighty was the creator of the universe, and this certainly involves an unqualified rejection of the theory of mechanistic evolution, which so dominates the thinking of non-Christian scientists today. The subsequent affirmation of the virgin birth of our Lord and Savior Jesus Christ likewise has a definite bearing on scientific theory today, for it is commonly thought that no events can take place in nature that do not constantly recur so as to be subject to scientific observation and analysis. Again, the bodily resurrection of Christ is both a scientific and a historical event, along with its theological importance for the salvation of sinners. Christ's sufferings and death on the cross under the authority of Pontius Pilate are likewise events in history. Therefore, if the Bible may have erred in its statements concerning history and science (interpreted, of course, in the way the original author intended them) the doctrinal or theological affirmations for which they form the framework must also be subject to error.

AUTHORITY OF THE OLD TESTAMENT

The Old Testament shows no awareness whatever of any supposed line of distinction between theological doctrine and miraculous events. This is true of the accounts of Moses' time, concerning both history and science. Psalm 105, composed four or five centuries after the Exodus, heartily reaffirms the historicity of the ten plagues on Egypt as recorded in Exodus 7–12, and renders thanks to the Lord for this display of his power in redeeming Israel from her bondage. Psalm 106 likewise exalts the name of Yahweh for the miraculous parting of the waters of the Red Sea and for the sudden destruction of Dathan and Abiram as they sought to set aside Moses and his revelation. These saving acts of God are referred to as factual episodes in the history of redemption. And so are the battle of Gibeon (which features the prolongation of the day and the destruction of the enemy by a catastrophic hailstorm) and the fall of the walls of Jericho at the sound of a trumpet blast (see Isa. 28:21; 1 Kings 16:34).

Ancient Israel was as sure of the reality of the Red Sea crossing as the apostolic church was of Christ's death on Calvary. So no matter how rationalists and antisupernaturalists scoff at these episodes as fabulous and nonhistorical, the Hebrew Scriptures themselves affirm them without qualification as actually having taken place on the plane of history.

Much more could be said concerning the testimony of Holy Scripture to its own plenary inspiration. One of the best discussions concerning these matters is to be found in chapter 2 of L. Gaussen's *Theopneustia: The Bible, Its Divine Origin and Inspiration*,[2] where he points to innumerable passages in the Old Testament that assert unequivocally that the words of the prophets were the words of God. Not only in the Pentateuch (Exod. 4:30; Deut. 18:21, 22, and the numberless instances in Leviticus) but also throughout the prophets we meet with such affirmations as "The LORD has spoken [the following words]," "The mouth of the LORD has spoken," "The word of the LORD came to _____ saying" (Josh. 24:2; Isa. 8:11; Jer 7:1; 11:1; 18:1; 21:1; 26:1; 27:1; 30:1, 4; 50:1; 51:12; Amos 3:1; *passim*).

Hosea begins, "The word of the LORD that came to Hosea. . . ." This fullness of inspiration is asserted of the Psalms as well: "Sovereign Lord, . . . who by the mouth of our father David, thy servant, didst say . . ." (Acts 4:24-26, quoting Ps. 2:1, 2). So also Peter says of David in connection with Psalm 16:10: "Being therefore a prophet, and knowing that God had sworn with an oath to him that he would set one of his descendants upon his throne, he foresaw and spoke of the resurrection of the Christ, that He was not abandoned to Hades, nor did His flesh see corruption" (Acts. 2:30, 31). Very clearly, then, God is here said to have spoken by the mouth of David, even though the actual speech and inscripturation were done by David himself. Second Peter 1:20 speaks of the Old Testament in general as the "prophecy of Scripture" *(prophēteia graphēs)* and clearly affirms that it did not come by the will of man (as if invented or thought up by the human author on his own initiative) but only as the human author was moved by the Holy Spirit and thus produced in his own human words exactly what God intended him to say. These inspired writings were truly the words of God (even though conveyed through the human instrumentality of the prophet) and contained a full and complete magisterial authority.

This authority is constantly recognized by the Gospel writers, who often remarked: "All this took place to fulfill what the Lord had spoken by the Prophet" (Matt. 1:22; cf. 2:5, 15, 23; 13:35;

21:4; 27:9, *passim).* As Gaussen points out, "Nowhere shall we find a single passage that permits us to detach one single part of it as less divine that all the rest."[3] That is, the distinction between the doctrinal-theological and the historical-scientific drawn by some modern writers on this subject is completely foreign to the attitude of the New Testament authors toward the Old.

CHRIST'S UNQUALIFIED ACCEPTANCE OF THE OLD TESTAMENT

Jesus of Nazareth clearly assumed the errorlessness of the Old Testament in all its statements and affirmations, even in the realms of history and science. In Matthew 19:4, 5 he affirmed that God himself spoke the words of Genesis 2:24, with reference to the literal, historical Adam and Eve, as he established the ordinance of marriage. In Matthew 23:35 he put the historicity of Abel's murder by Cain on the same plane of historical factuality as the murder of Zechariah the son of Barachiah. In Matthew 24:38, 39 Jesus clearly accepted the historicity of the universal flood and Noah's ark: "For as in those days before the flood they were eating and drinking, marrying and giving in marriage, until the day when Noah entered the ark, and they did not know until the flood came and swept them all away. . . ." This record, bearing upon both history and science, has been scornfully rejected by those who trust in the infallible accuracy of modern scientific empiricism.

The same is true of the account of the prophet Jonah's preservation from drowning through the agency of a great fish that three days later spewed him forth on the shore. Yet Jesus put his crucifixion and resurrection on the same historical plane, saying, "For as Jonah was three days and three nights in the belly of the whale, so will the Son of man be three days and three nights in the heart of the earth" (Matt. 12:40). In the same way, Christ goes on in the very next verse to confirm that the heathen population of Nineveh really did repent at the preaching of Jonah, just as recorded in Jonah 3:7-9. Even though this account has been treated with skepticism by modern scholarship, the New Testament indicates that Jesus regarded it as sober fact.

In the light of these passages, it seems clear that Jesus regarded the Hebrew Bible as completely trustworthy and reliable in all that it affirms in matters of theology, history, and science.

This conclusion carries with it a corollary that renders indefensible the view that the inerrancy of Scripture extends only to its doctrinal teaching. The New Testament teaches that Jesus Christ is the incarnate God. For example, John 1:14 proclaims him the eternal Word who at the Incarnation became flesh and dwelt among men as Jesus of Nazareth. If, then, Jesus was mistaken in regarding the Old Testament as completely trustworthy, reliable, and inerrant in matters of doctrine, history, and science, it must follow that God himself was mistaken about the inerrancy of the Hebrew Scriptures. And the proposition that God was mistaken is surely a theological issue if there ever was one! It turns out, then, that errancy in matters of history and science leads inevitably to errancy in matters (and very important matters!) of theology as well. Once the dike has been breached, it is eventually washed away.

Some have suggested that Jesus was actually aware of the true authorship and date of composition of the various books of the Old Testament, and that he had personal knowledge of the historical and scientific mistakes embedded in the Hebrew Scriptures. Nevertheless, for the sake of more effective teaching in the area of theology or ethics he found it best to accommodate himself to the widely accepted views of his contemporaries. In other words, he pretended that Moses had personally written all the Pentateuch under inspiration, that Adam and Eve were actual historical persons, that Noah's flood took place exactly as described in Genesis 6–9, that Jonah was swallowed by a great fish and later expelled by it on the shore of the sea—even though he knew these events were not actually true. In order to avoid unimportant "side-issues" of authenticity and accuracy on these secondary levels, he simply went along with public opinion while presenting his doctrinal teaching. This interpretation of Jesus and his treatment of higher critical issues finds special favor in certain liberal Roman Catholic circles.

Yet when subjected to logical scrutiny, it must be recognized that this view is impossible to reconcile with the truthfulness and holiness of God. If Jesus of Nazareth knew that the story of Jonah's deliverance through the fish was altogether fictitious, he could never have used it as a historical type of the experience of burial and resurrection that he himself was shortly to undergo. This kind of accommodation would have bordered on the duplicity employed by unscrupulous politicians in the heat of an election campaign. But in contrast to this, Jesus made plain to his hearers that "he who sent me is true, and I declare to the world what I have heard from him" (John 8:26). Again, "I speak of what I have seen with my Father" (John 8:38). The words of Jesus were the words of God, and the God who pronounced judgment on false-hood could not himself have resorted to falsehood in the procla-mation of his saving truth.

There is a further serious objection to this theory of accommo-dation. The four Gospels make plain that Jesus refused to ac-commodate himself to certain mistaken views current in his own time. Take, for example, his repeated affirmation in the Sermon on the Mount: "You have heard that it was said to the men of old . . . But *I* say to you. . ." (Matt. 5). Or again, the remarkable statements in John 8:24 ("I told you that you would die in your sins, . . . you will die in your sins unless you believe that I am he") and John 8:44 ("You are of your father the devil"). Nothing could be farther from accommodation to popular opinion than this. The same is true of his strict position concerning divorce (Matt. 19:9) and allegedly non-binding oaths (Matt. 23:16-22) and his downgrading of the importance of kosher restrictions concerning foods in favor of that which controls the motives and attitudes of the heart (Matt. 15:11-20). Jesus never stooped to accommoda-tion in order to ingratiate himself with his public. As Peter affirmed of him, "He committed no sin; no guile was found on his lips" (1 Peter 2:22).

INERRANCY ESSENTIAL FOR BIBLICAL AUTHORITY

We are faced with a basic choice in the matter of biblical authority. Either we receive the Scripture as completely reliable and trustworthy in every matter it records, affirms, or teaches, or else it comes to us as a collection of religious writings containing both truth and error.

If it does contain mistakes in the original manuscripts, then it ceases to be unconditionally authoritative. It must be validated and endorsed by our own human judgment before we can accept it as true. It is not sufficient to establish that a matter has been affirmed or taught in Scripture; it may nevertheless be mistaken and at variance with the truth. So human judges must pass on each item of teaching or information contained in the Bible and determine whether it is actually to be received as true. Such judgment presupposes a superior wisdom and spiritual insight competent to correct the errors of the Bible, and if those who would thus judge the veracity of the Bible lack the necessary ingredient of personal inerrancy in judgment, they may come to a false and mistaken judgment—endorsing as true what is actually false, or else condemning as erroneous what is actually correct in Scripture. Thus the objective authority of the Bible is replaced by a subjective intuition or judicial faculty on the part of each believer, and it becomes a matter of mere personal preference how much of Scripture teaching he or she may adopt as binding.

In contrast to the view of the Bible as capable of error in matters of science, history, or doctrine (certainly such doctrine as is contained in a historical or scientific framework), we find that the attitude of Christ and the apostolic authors of the New Testament was one of unqualified acceptance. Christ may have illumined the basic intention of the Ten Commandments by setting forth their spiritual implications ("But *I* say to you . . ."), but never did he suggest that any affirmation or teaching in the Old Testament required validation by modern critical scholarship. He clearly presupposed that whatever the Old Testament taught was true because it was the infallible Word of God. It needed no further screening process by human wisdom in order to be verified. "For truly, I say to you," said Jesus, "till heaven and earth pass away, not an iota, not a dot, will pass from the law [Old Testament] until all is accomplished" (Matt. 5:18). His statement in John 10:35, "The Scripture cannot be broken," carries the same implication.

Those apostolic authors whom he taught or inspired proclaim the same full authority of all Scripture. Paul says in 2 Timothy 3:16: "All Scripture is inspired by God and profitable for teaching, for reproof, for correction, and for training in righteousness." In Hebrews 1:1, 2 we read, "God spoke of old to our fathers by the prophets; but in these last days he has spoken to us by a Son." This asserts the same infallibility for the writings of the Old Testament as for the words of Jesus himself. In 1 Peter 1:10, 11 the apostle states: "The prophets who prophesied of the grace that was to be yours searched and inquired about this salvation; they inquired what person or time was indicated by the Spirit of Christ within them when predicting the sufferings of Christ and the subsequent glory." This clearly implies that the Holy Spirit was within the Old Testament authors as they composed the books of the Hebrew Scriptures and that he guided them into words of infallible truth sure of fulfillment, even though the human authors themselves may not have fully understood all that these words predicted. Especially instructive is 2 Peter 1:20, 21: "First of all you must understand this, that no prophecy of scripture is a matter of one's own interpretation, because no prophecy ever came by the impulse of man, but men moved by the Holy Spirit spoke from God." As they wrote down God's revelation, the Old Testament authors were supernaturally borne along (like sailing vessels impelled by the wind, *pheromenoi)* to record God's truth, which is not to be manipulated or perverted by one's own personal interpretation or preference. Despite all the imperfections of the human writers of Scripture, the Lord was able to carry them along into his infallible truth without distortion or mistake.

Both Christ and the apostles affirm, then, that what the Bible says, God says. All these passages add up to this: that accuracy inheres in every part of the Bible, so that it is to be received as infallible as to truth and final as to authority. When the Scripture speaks, it speaks as the living, operative Word of God (Heb. 4:12—*zōn* and *energēs),* which penetrates to man's innermost being and sits in judgment on all human philosophies and reasonings with an authority that is absolutely sovereign. This, then, is what the Scriptures teach concerning their own infallibility. Not only are they free from all error; they are also filled with all authority, and they sit in judgment on man and all his intentions and thoughts.

This objective authority of the Bible carries with it an important consequence as to its interpretation. Scripture must never be construed according to a man's personal preference or bias just to suit his own purposes. It must be carefully and reverently studied with a view to ascertaining what the human biblical author (guided by the divine Author) intended by the words he used. This makes historico-grammatical exegesis an absolute necessity. We fall into misinterpretation when we err in understanding the Hebrew or Greek words that compose the original Scripture itself, supposing them to mean something the ancient writer never intended, simply because the English words of our Bible translations might be so construed. We grievously err in our interpretation when we interpret figurative language literally; we likewise err when we interpret literal language figuratively.

The authority of Scripture requires that in whatever the author meant to say by the words he used, he presents us with the truth of God, without any admixture of error. As such it is binding on our minds and consciences, and we can reject or evade its teaching only at the peril of our souls.

OLD TESTAMENT QUOTATIONS IN THE NEW TESTAMENT

It has often been observed by careful students of the Bible that a certain number of the Old Testament passages quoted in the New are not quoted with literal exactness. Often this is accounted for by the fact that a completely literal translation of Hebrew does not make clear sense in Greek, and therefore some minor adjustments must be made for the sake of good communication. But there are a few instances where the rewording amounts to a sort of loose paraphrase. Particularly is this true in the case of quotations from the Septuagint (the translation into Greek of the entire Old Testament by Jewish scholars in Alexandria, Egypt, during the third and second centuries B.C.). For the most part, the Septuagint is quite faithful to the Hebrew wording in the Old Testament, but in a small number of instances there are noticeable deviations in the mode of expressing the thought, even though there may be no essential difference in the thought itself.

Some scholars have drawn the conclusion from such deviations that the New Testament authors could not have held to the theory of verbal inspiration; otherwise they would have gone back to the Hebrew text and done a meticulously exact translation of their own as they rendered that text into Greek. It has even been argued that the occasional use of an inexact Septuagint rendering in a New Testament quotation demonstrates a rejection of inerrancy on the part of the apostolic authors themselves. Their inclusion of the Septuagint quotations that contain elements of inexactitude would seem to indicate a cavalier attitude toward the whole matter of inerrancy. On the basis of inference from the phenomena of Scripture itself, it is therefore argued that the Bible makes no claim to inerrancy.

To this line of reasoning we make the following reply. The very reason for using the Septuagint was rooted in the missionary outreach of the evangelists and apostles of the early church. The Septuagint translation of the Old Testament had already found its way into every city of the Roman Empire to which the Jews of the Dispersion had gone. This was virtually the only form of the Old Testament in the hands of Jewish believers outside Palestine, and it was certainly the only form available for gentile converts to the Jewish faith or Christianity. The apostles were propagating a Gospel that presented Jesus Christ as the fulfillment of the messianic promises of the Old Testament. Their audiences throughout the Near East and the Mediterranean world were told that they had only to consult the Old Testament to verify the truth of the apostolic claims that Jesus in his person and by his work had fulfilled the promises of God. Had the New Testament authors quoted these promises in any other form than the wording of the Septuagint, they would have engendered uncertainty and doubt in the minds of their hearers. For as they checked their Old Testament, the readers would have noticed the discrepancies at once—minor though they may have been—and they would with one voice have objected, "But that isn't the way I read it in my Bible!" The apostles and their Jewish co-workers from Palestine may have been well-equipped to do their own original translation from the Hebrew original. But they would have been ill-advised to substitute their own more literal rendering for that form of the Old Testament that was already in the hands of their public. They really had little choice but to keep largely to the Septuagint in all their quotations of the Old Testament.

On the other hand, the special Hebrew-Christian audience to which the evangelist Matthew addressed himself—and even more notably the recipients of the Epistle to the Hebrews—did not require such a constant adherence to the Septuagint as was necessary for a gentile readership. Hence Matthew and Hebrews often quote from the Old Testament in a non-Septuagintal form, normally in a form somewhat closer to the wording of the Hebrew original. And it should also be observed that in some cases, at least, these Greek renderings (whether Septuagintal or not) point to a variant reading in the original form of the text that is better than the one that has come down to us in the standard Hebrew Bible. It should be carefully noted that none of this yields any evidence whatever of carelessness or disregard on the part of the apostles in respect to the exact wording of the original Hebrew. Far from it. In some instances Christ himself based his teaching on a careful exegesis of the exact reading in the Torah. For example, he pointed out in Matthew 22:32 the implications of Exodus 3:6 ("I *am* the God of Abraham, and the God of Isaac, and the God of Jacob") on the basis of the present tense implied by the verbless clause in Hebrew. He declared that God would not have spoken of himself as the God of mere corpses moldering in the grave ("He is not God of the dead, but of the living"). Therefore Abraham, Isaac, and Jacob must have been alive and well in the life beyond at the time when God addressed Moses at the burning bush four or five centures after they had died. Similarly his discussion with the Pharisees concerning the identity of the one referred to as "my lord" in Psalm 110:1 really turned upon the exact terms used in that clause or sentence. He therefore asked them, "If David thus calls him Lord, how is he his son?" (Matt. 22:45). In other words, the Messiah must not only be David's lineal descendant, but he must also be his divine Lord (*kyrios*)!

Returning, then, to the apostolic use of the Septuagint, we find that this line of reasoning (that inexact quotations imply a low view of the Bible) is really without foundation. All of us employ standard translations of the Bible in our teaching and preaching, even those of us who are thoroughly conversant with the Greek and Hebrew originals of Scripture. But our use of any translation in English, French, or any other modern language by no means implies that we have abandoned a belief in Scriptural inerrancy, even though some errors of translation appear in every one of those modern versions. We use these standard translations in order to teach our readership in terms they can verify from the Bibles they have in their own homes. But most of us are careful to point out to them that the only final authority as to the meaning of Scripture is the wording of the original languages themselves. There is no infallible translation. But this involves no surrender of the conviction that the original manuscripts of Scripture were free from all error. We must therefore conclude that the New Testament use of the Septuagint implies nothing against verbal inspiration or Scriptural inerrancy.

In the light of the foregoing discussion, we are left with no defensible middle ground. No reasonable alternative is left but to reduce the Bible to the status of a mixture of truth and error requiring the validation of its truth by human reason or else to take our stand with Jesus Christ and the apostles in a full acceptance of the infallible, inerrant authority of the original autographs.

Notes

[1]Frederick G. Kenyon, *Recent Developments in the Textual Criticism of the Greek Bible* (New York and London: Oxford University Press, 1933), pp. 74-76.

[2]L. Gaussen, *Theopneustia: The Bible, Its Divine Origin and Inspiration,* trans. by David D. Scott (Cincinnati, Boston, and New York: Blanchard, 1859).

[3]Ibid, p. 67.

SOLA SCRIPTURA:
CRUCIAL TO EVANGELICALISM

R.C. Sproul

R.C. Sproul is Director and Staff Theologian, Ligonier Valley Study Center near Stahlstown in western Pennsylvania. He is a graduate of Westminster College, B.A.; Pittsburgh Theological Seminary, B.D.; and the Free University of Amsterdam, Drs. He holds an honorary doctorate from Geneva College, Litt.D. He has served on the faculties of Westminster College, Gordon College, and the Conwell School of Theology and was formerly Minister of Theology at the College Hill United Presbyterian Church, Cincinnati, Ohio. He is a minister in the Presbyterian Church in America; Visiting Professor at Trinity Episcopal Seminary, Sewickley, Pennsylvania; and Visiting Professor of Apologetics at Gordon-Conwell Theological Seminary, South Hamilton, Massachusetts. Dr. Sproul is the author of the following books and articles: The Symbol; The Psychology of Atheism; Discovering the Intimate Marriage; Knowing Scripture; Objections Answered; Soli Deo Gloria, *editor; and "The Case for Inerrancy: A Methodological Analysis" in* God's Inerrant Word, *edited by J.W. Montgomery.*

4 *R.C. Sproul*

SOLA SCRIPTURA:
CRUCIAL TO EVANGELICALISM

T HE ONLY source and norm of all Christian knowledge is the Holy Scripture."[1] This thematic statement introduces *De Scriptura Sacra* of Heinrich Heppe's classic work in Reformed dogmatics and provides a succinct expression of the Reformation slogan: *Sola Scriptura*. The two key words that are used to crystallize the *sola* character of Scripture are *source* and *norm*.

The Reformation principle of *Sola Scriptura* was given the status of the formal cause of the Reformation by Melanchthon and his Lutheran followers. The formal cause was distinguished from the material cause of *Sola Fide* (by faith alone). Though the chief theological issue of the Reformation was the question of the matter of justification, the controversy touched heavily on the underlying question of authority. As is usually the case in theological controversy, the issue of ultimate authority lurked in the background (though it was by no means hidden or obscure) of Luther's struggle with Rome over justification. The question of the *source* of Luther's doctrine and the normative authority by which it was to be judged was vital to his cause.

Sola Scriptura AND Inerrancy

A brief historical recapitulation of the steps that led to Luther's *Sola Scriptura* dictum may be helpful. After Luther posted his Ninety-Five Theses in 1517, a series of debates, correspondence, charges, and countercharges ensued, culminating in Luther's dramatic stand at Worms in April 1521. The two most significant transitional points between the theses of 1517 and the Diet of Worms of 1521 were the debates at Augsburg and Leipzig.

In October 1518 Luther met with Cardinal Cajetan of the Dominicans. Cajetan was acknowledged to be the most learned theologian of the Roman Curia. In the course of their discussions Cajetan was able to elicit from Luther his views on the infallibility of the pope. Luther asserted that the pope could err and claimed that Pope Clement VI's bull *Unigenitus* (1343) was contrary to Scripture.[2]

In the summer of 1519 the dramatic encounter between Luther and Johannes von Eck took place at Leipzig. In this exchange Eck elicited from Luther the admission of his belief that not only could the pope err but church councils could and did err as well. It was at Leipzig that Luther made clear his assertion: Scripture alone is the ultimate, divine authority in all matters pertaining to religion. Gordon Rupp gives the following account:

> Luther affirmed that "among the articles of John Huss and the Hussites which were condemned, are many which are truly Christian and evangelical, and which the church universal cannot condemn!" This was sensational! There was a moment of shocked silence, and then an uproar above which could be heard Duke George's disgusted, "Gad, Sir, that's the Plague! . . ." Eck pressed his advantage home, and Luther, trapped, admitted that since their decrees are also of human law, Councils may err.[3]

So by the time Luther stood before the Diet of Worms, the principle of *Sola Scriptura* was already well established in his mind and work. Only the Scripture carries absolute normative authority. Why? For Luther the *sola* of *Sola Scriptura* was inseparably related to the Scriptures' unique inerrancy. It was because popes could and did err and because councils could and did err that Luther came to realize the supremacy of Scripture. Luther did not despise chuch authority nor did he repudiate church councils as having no value. His praise of the Council of Nicea is noteworthy. Luther and the Reformers did not mean by *Sola Scriptura* that the Bible is the only authority in the church. Rather, they meant that the Bible is the only *infallible* authority in the church. Paul Althaus summarizes the train of Luther's thought by saying:

> We may trust unconditionally only in the Word of God and not in the teaching of the fathers; for the teachers of the Church can err

and have erred. Scripture never errs. Therefore it alone has un-conditional authority. The authority of the theologians of the Church is relative and conditional. Without the authority of the words of Scripture, no one can establish hard and fast statements in the Church.[4]

Thus Althaus sees Luther's principle of *Sola Scriptura* arising as a corollary of the inerrancy of Scripture. To be sure, the fact that Scripture is elevated to be the sole authority of the church does not carry with it the necessary inference that it is inerrant. It could be asserted that councils, popes, and the Bible all err[5] and still postulate a theory of *Sola Scriptura*. Scripture could be considered on a *primus inter pares* ("first among equals") basis with ecclesiastical authority, giving it a kind of primacy among errant sources. Or Scripture could be regarded as carrying unique authority solely on the basis of its being the primary historical source of the gospel. But the Reformers' view of *Sola Scriptura* was higher than this. The Reformation principle of *Sola Scriptura* involved inerrancy.[6]

Sola Scriptura, ascribing to the Scriptures a unique authority, must be understood in a normative sense. Not descriptive, but rather normative authority is meant by the formula. The normative character of the *Sola Scriptura* principle may be seen by a brief survey of sixteenth-century Reformed confessions.[7] The Theses of Berne (1528):

> The Church of Christ makes no laws or commandments without God's Word. Hence all human traditions, which are called ecclesiastical commandments, are binding upon us only in so far as they are based on and commanded by God's Word (Sec. II).

The Geneva Confession (1536):

> First we affirm that we desire to follow Scripture alone as a rule of faith and religion, without mixing with it any other things which might be devised by the opinion of men apart from the Word of God, and without wishing to accept for our spiritual government any other doctrine than what is conveyed to us by the same Word without addition or diminution, according to the command of our Lord (Sec. I).

The French Confession of Faith (1559):

> We believe that the Word contained in these books has proceeded from God, and receives its authority from him alone, and not from men. And inasmuch as it is the rule of all truth, containing all that

is necessary for the service of God and for our salvation, it is not lawful for men, nor even for angels, to add to it, to take away from it, or to change it. Whence it follows that no authority, whether of antiquity, or custom, or numbers, or human wisdom, or judgments, or proclamations, or edicts, or decrees, or councils, or visions, or miracles, should be opposed to these Holy Scriptures, but on the contrary, all things should be examined, regulated, and reformed according to them (Art. V).

The Belgic Confession (1561):

We receive all these books, and these only, as holy and confirmation of our faith; believing, without any doubt, all things contained in them, not so much because the church receives and approves them as such, but more especially because the Holy Ghost witnessed in our hearts that they are from God, whereof they carry the evidence in themselves (Art. V).

Therefore we reject with all our hearts whatsoever doth not agree with this infallible rule (Art. VII).

Second Helvetic Confession (1566):

Therefore, we do not admit any other judge than Christ himself, who proclaims by the Holy Scriptures what is true, what is false, what is to be followed, or what is to be avoided (Chap. II).

Uniformly the sixteenty-century confessions elevate the authority of Scripture over any other conceivable authority. Thus, even the testimony of angels is to be judged by the Scriptures. Why? Because, as Luther believed, the Scriptures alone are inerrant. *Sola Scriptura* as the supreme norm of ecclesiastical authority rests ultimately on the premise of the infallibility of the Word of God.

EXTENT OF THE NORM

To what extent does the *Sola Scriptura* principle of authority apply? We hear statements that declare Scripture to be the "only infallible rule of faith and practice." Does this limit the scope of biblical infallibility? Among advocates of limited inerrancy we hear the popular notion that the Bible is inerrant or infallible only when it speaks of matters of faith and practice. Matters of history or cosmology may contain error, but not matters of faith and practice. Here we see a subtle shift from the Reformation principle. Note the difference in the following propositions:

A. The Bible is the only infallible rule of faith and practice.
B. The Bible is infallible only when it speaks of faith and practice.

In premise A, "faith and practice" are generic terms that describe the Bible. In premise B, "faith and practice" presumably describe only a particular part of the Bible. Premise A affirms that there is but one infallible authority for the church. The proposition sets no content limit on the infallibility of the Scriptures. Premise B gives a reduced canon of that which is infallible; that is, the Bible is infallible only when it speaks of faith and practice. This second premise represents a clear and decisive departure from the Reformation view.

Premise A does not say that the Bible provides information about every area of life, such as mathematics or physics. But it affirms that what the Bible teaches, it teaches infallibly.

THE SOURCE OF AUTHORITY

Heppe's *sola* indicates that the Bible is not only the unique and final authority of the church but is also the "only source of all Christian knowledge." At first glance this statement may seem to suggest that the only source of revelation open to man is that found in Scripture. But that is not the intent of Heppe's statement, nor is it the intent of the Reformation principle of *Sola Scriptura.*

Uniformly the Reformers acknowledged general revelation as a source of knowledge of God. The question of whether or not that general revelation yields a bona fide natural theology was and is widely disputed, but there is no serious doubt that the Reformers affirmed a revelation present in nature.[8] Thus the *sola* does not exclude general revelation but points beyond it to the sufficiency of Scripture as the unique source of written special revelation.

The context of the *Sola Scriptura* schema with respect to source was the issue (raised over against Rome) regarding the relationship of Scripture and Tradition. Central to the debate was the Council of Trent's declaration regarding Scripture and Tradition. (Trent was part of the Roman counteroffensive to the Reformation, and *Sola Scriptura* was not passed over lightly in this counteroffensive.) In the Fourth Session of the Council of Trent the following decree was formulated:

> This (Gospel), of old promised through the Prophets in the Holy Scriptures, our Lord Jesus Christ, the Son of God, promulgated first with His own mouth, and then commanded it to be preached by His Apostles to every creature as the source at once of all saving truth and rules of conduct. It also clearly perceives that these

truths and rules are contained *in the written books and in the unwritten traditions,* which, received by the Apostles from the mouth of Christ Himself, or from the Apostles themselves, the Holy Ghost dictating, have come down to us, transmitted as it were from hand to hand. Following then, the examples of the Orthodox fathers, it receives and venerates with a feeling of piety and reverence all the books both of the Old and New Testaments, since one God is the author of both; also the traditions, whether they relate to faith or to morals, as having been dictated either orally by Christ or by the Holy Ghost, and preserved in the Catholic church in unbroken succession.[9]

In this decree the Roman Catholic church apparently affirmed *two* sources of special revelation—Scripture and the Tradition of the church—although in recent years this "dual source" theory has come into question within the Roman church.

G.C. Berkouwer's work on Vatican Council II provides a lengthy discussion of current interpretations of the Tridentine formula on Scripture and Tradition. Some scholars argue that Tradition adds no new content to Scripture but merely serves either as a depository in the life of the church or as a formal interpretive tool of the church.[10] A technical point of historical research concerning Trent sheds some interesting light on the matter. In the original draft of the fourth session of Trent the decree read that "the truths . . . are contained partly [*partim*] in Scripture and partly [*partim*] in the unwritten traditions." But at a decisive point in the Council's deliberations two priests, Nacchianti and Bonnucio rose in protest against the *partim . . . partim* formula. These men protested on the grounds that this view would destroy the uniqueness and sufficiency of Scripture.[11] All we know from that point on is that the words *partly . . . partly* were removed from the text and replaced by the word *and* (*et*). Did this mean that the Council responded to the protest and perhaps left the relationship between Scripture and Tradition purposely ambiguous? Was the change stylistic, meaning that the Council still maintained two distinct sources of revelation? These questions are the focus of the current debate among Roman theologians.

One thing is certain. The Roman church has interpreted Trent as affirming two sources of special revelation since the sixteenth century. Vatican I spoke of two sources. The papal encyclical *Humani Generis* spoke of "sources of revelation."[12] Even Pope John XXIII spoke of Scripture *and* Tradition in *Ad Petri Cathedram.*[13]

Not only has the dual-source theory been confirmed both by

ecumenical councils and papal encyclicals, but tradition has been appealed to on countless occasions to validate doctrinal formulations that divide Rome and Protestantism. This is particularly true regarding decisions in the area of Mariology.

Over against this dual-source theory stands the *sola* of *Sola Scriptura.* Again, the Reformers did not despise the treasury of church tradition. The great councils of Nicea, Ephesus, Chalcedon, and Constantinople receive much honor in Protestant tradition. The Reformers themselves gave tribute to the insights of the church fathers. Calvin's love for Augustine is apparent throughout the *Institutes.* Luther's expertise in the area of Patristics was evident in his debates with Cajetan and Eck. He frequently quotes the fathers as highly respected ecclesiastical authorities. But the difference is this: For the Reformers no church council, synod, classical theologian, or early church father is regarded as infallible. All are open to correction and critique. We have no *Doctor Irrefragabilis* of Protestantism.

Protestant churches have tended to be confessional in character. Subscription to confessions and creeds has been mandatory for the clergy and parish of many demonimations. Confessions have been used as a test of orthodoxy and conformity to the faith and practice of the church. But the confessions are all regarded as reformable. They are considered reformable because they are considered fallible. But the *Sola Scriptura* principles in its classic application regards the Scripture as irreformable because of its infallibility.

Thus the two primary thrusts of *Sola Scriptura* point to: 1) Scripture's uniqueness as normative authority and 2) its uniqueness as the source of special revelation. Norm and source are the twin implicates of the *Sola Scriptura* principle.

IS *SOLA SCRIPTURA* THE ESSENCE OF CHRISTIANITY?

In a recent publication on questions of Scripture, Bernard Ramm wrote an essay entitled, "Is 'Scripture Alone' the Essence of Christianity?" Using the nineteenth-century German penchant for the quest of the *"Wesen"* of Christianity as a jumping-off point, Ramm gives a brief history of the liberal-conservative controversy concerning the role of Scripture in the Christian faith. Defining *Wesen* as "the essence of something, the real spirit or burden of a treatise, the heart of the matter," he concludes that Scripture is not the *Wesen* of Christianity. He provides a historical survey to indicate that neither the Reformers nor the strong advocates of inerrancy, A.A. Hodge and B.B. Warfield, believed that *Sola Scriptura* was the essence of Christianity. Ramm cites numerous quotations from Hodge and Warfield that speak of the Scriptures as being "absolutely infallible," and "without error of facts or doctrines." Yet these men affirmed that "Christianity was true independently of any theory of inspiration, and its great doctrines were believable within themselves."[14]

Ramm goes on to express grave concern about the present debate among evangelicals concerning inerrancy. Here his concern focuses not on the teaching of Hodge and Warfield but on the attitudes of their contemporary disciples who, in Ramm's opinion, go beyond their forefathers in asserting a particular view of Scripture as being Christianity's essence. Ramm writes:

> From the other writings of Warfield in particular, it would be impossible to say that he identified the *Wesen* of Christianity with his view of Holy Scripture. He was enough of a historian of theology to avoid saying that. The "inspiration" article was an essay in strategy. However, among current followers of the so-called Warfield position there have been certain shifts away from the original strategic stance of the essay. One's doctrine of Scripture has become now the first and most important doctrine, one's theory of the *Wesen* of Christianity, so that all other doctrines have validity now only as they are part of the inerrant Scripture. Thus evangelical teachers, or evangelical schools or evangelical movements, can be judged as to whether or not they are true to the *Wesen* of Christianity by their theory of inspiration. It can be stated even more directly: an evangelical has made a theory of inspiration the *Wesen* of Christianity if he assumes that the most important doctrine in a man's theology, and most revelatory of the entire range of his theological thought, is his theology of inspiration.[15]

It appears from this statement that the "essence" of Ramm's concern for the present state of evangelicalism is that one's doctrine of Scripture is viewed as the essence or *Wesen* of Christianity. This writer can only join hands with Ramm in total agreement with his concern. To make one's view of Scripture in general or of inspiration in particular the essence of Christianity would be to commit an error of the most severe magnitude. To subordinate the importance of the gospel itself to the importance of our historical source book of it would be to obscure the centrality of Christ. To subordinate *Sola Fide* to *Sola Scriptura* would be to misunderstand radically the *Wesen* of the Reformation. Clearly Ramm is correct in taking his stand on this point with Hodge, Warfield, and the Reformers. Who can object to that?

One may be troubled, however, by a portion of Ramm's stated concern. Who are these "current followers" of Warfield who in fact do maintain that *Sola Scriptura* is the heart or essence of Christianity? What disciple of Warfield's has ever maintained that *Sola Scriptura* is essential to salvation? Ramm provides us with no names or documentary evidence to demonstrate that his deep concern is warranted.

To be sure, strong statements have been made by followers of the Warfield school of the crucial importance of *Sola Scriptura* and the centrality of biblical authority to all theological disputes. Perhaps these statements have contained some "overkill" in the passion of debate, which is always regrettable. We must be very cautious in our zeal to defend a high view of Scripture not to give the impression that we are talking about an article on which our salvation depends.[16]

We can cite the following statements by advocates of the Warfield school that could be construed as a possible basis for Ramm's concern. In *God's Inerrant Word*, J.I. Packer makes the following assertion:

> What Luther thus voiced at Worms shows the essential motivation and concern, theological and religious, of the entire Reformation movement: namely that the Word of God alone must rule, and no Christian man dare do other than allow it to enthrone itself in his conscience and heart.[17]

Here Packer calls the notion of *Sola Scriptura* "the essential motivation and concern" of the Reformation. In itself this quote certainly suggests that Packer views *Sola Scriptura* as *the* essence of the Reformation.

However, in defense of Packer it must be noted that to say *Sola Scriptura* was the essential motivation of the Reformation movement is not to say that *Sola Scriptura* is the essence of Christianity. He is speaking here of a historical controversy. That *Sola Scriptura* was at the heart of the controversy and central to the debate cannot be doubted. To say that *Sola Scriptura* was *an* essential motif or concern of the Reformation cannot be doubted. That it was *the essential* concern may be brought into question; this may be regarded as an overstatement. But again, in fairness to Packer, it must be noted that earlier in his essay he had already indicated that Justification by Faith Alone was the material principle. So he had already maintained that *Sola Scriptura* was subordinate to *Sola Fide* in the controversy.[18] In any case, though the word *essential* is used, there is no hint here that Packer maintains that *Sola Scriptura* is *the* essence of Christianity.

In a recent unpublished essay, Richard Lovelace of Gordon-Conwell Theological Seminary cites both Harold Lindsell and Francis Schaeffer as men who have sounded urgent warnings concering the relationship between inerrancy and evangelicalism. Lovelace cites the following statements of Schaeffer:

> There is no use of evafigelicalism seeming to get larger and larger, if at the same time appreciable parts . . . are getting soft at that which is the central core, namely the Scriptures. . . . We must . . . say most lovingly but clearly: evangelicalism is not consistently evangelical unless there is a line drawn between those who take a full view of Scripture and those who do not.[19]

Again Schaeffer is cited: "Holding to a strong view of Scripture or not holding to it is the watershed of the evangelical world."[20] In these statements Francis Schaeffer maintains that the Scriptures are: 1) the "central core" of evangelicalism, 2) a mark of "consistent evangelicalism," and 3) the "watershed of the evangelical world." These are strong assertions about the role of *Sola Scriptura*, but they are made with reference to evangelicalism, not Christianity (though I am sure Schaeffer believes evangelicalism is the purest expression of Christianity to be found). Evangelicalism refers to a historical position or movement. When he speaks of "watersheds," he is speaking of crucial historical turning points. When he speaks of "consistent" evangelicalism, he implies there may be such a thing as inconsistent evangelicalism.

The troublesome quote of Schaeffer is that one in which he says the Scriptures are "the central core" of evangelicalism. Here "core" is in the singular with the definite article giving it a *sola* character. Does Schaeffer mean that the Bible is the core of evangelicalism and the gospel is the husk? Is *Sola Scriptura* the center and *Sola Fide* at the periphery of evangelicalism? It is hard to think that Schaeffer would make such an assertion. Indeed, one may question if Schaeffer means what he in fact does say here. Had he said, "Scripture is *at* the core of evangelicalism," there would be no dispute. But to say it *is* the core appears an over-statement. Perhaps we have here a slip of the pen, which any of us can and frequently do make.

In similar fashion Harold Lindsell may be quoted: "Is the term 'evangelical' broad enough in its meaning to include within it believers in inerrancy and believers in an inerrancy limited to matters of faith and practice?"[21] Lindsell raises the question of whether or not inerrancy of the entire Bible is essential to the term *evangelical.* The question raised is: If *Sola Scriptura* in its fullest sense is of the *Wesen* of evangelicalism, can one who espouses limited inerrancy be genuinely called evangelical? The issue is the meaning of the term evangelical. Does it carry with it the automatic assumption of full inerrancy? Again we must point out the difference between the historical label "evangelical" and what is essential to Christianity.

None of the scholars mentioned have said that adherence to inerrancy or *Sola Scriptura* is essential to salvation. None have *Sola Scriptura* as the *Wesen* of Christianity.

It could be said that the argument of the writer of this chapter is constructed on straw men who "come close" to asserting that *Sola Scriptura* is the essence of Christianity but who, in the final analysis, shrink from such an assertion. But it is not my purpose to create straw men. It is simply to find some basis for Ramm's assertion about modern followers of Warfield. Since I have not been able to find any followers of Warfield who assert *Sola Scriptura* as the *Wesen* of Christianity, the best I can do is to cite examples of statements that could possibly be misconstrued to assert that. It is probably charity that restrained Ramm from naming those he had in mind. But unfortunately, the absence of names casts a shadow of suspicion over all modern followers of Warfield who hold to full inerrancy.

Though advocates of inerrancy in the full sense of *Sola Scriptura* do not regard it as being essential to salvation, they do maintain that the principle is *crucial* to Christianity and to consistent evangelicalism. That in Scripture we have divine revelation is no small matter. That the gospel rests not on human conjecture or rational speculation is of vital importance. But there is no quarrel with Ramm on these points. He summarizes his own position by saying:

1. There is no questioning of the *Sola Scriptura* in theology. Scripture is the supreme and final authority in theological decision-making.

2. One's views of revelation, inspiration, and interpretation are important. They do implicate each other. Our discussion rather has been whether a certain view of inspiration could stand as the *Wesen* of Christianity. We have in no manner suggested that mat-

ters of revelation, inspiration, and interpretation are unimportant in theology.[22]

Here we delight in agreement with this strong affirmation of the crucial importance of *Sola Scriptura*.

Strangely, however, Ramm continues his summary by saying, "If the integrity of other evangelicals, evangelical schools, or evangelical movements are assessed by their view of inspiration, then, for them, inspiration has become the *Wesen* of Christianity."[23] The inference Ramm draws at this point is at once puzzling and astonishing, and perhaps we meet here merely another case of overstatement or a slip of the pen. How would it follow from an assessment of others' evangelicalism as being consistent or inconsistent according to their view of Scripture that inspiration has become the *Wesen* of Christianity? This inference involves a quantum leap of logic.

If the first two points of Ramm's summary are correct—that *Sola Scriptura* is important and that it implicates views of interpretation and theological decision making—why should not a school's or movement's integrity (a fully integrated stance) be assessed by this principle? Though *Sola Scriptura* is not the *Wesen* of Christianity, it is still of crucial importance. If a school or movement softens its view of Scripture, that does not mean it has repudiated the essence of Christianity. But it does mean that a crucial point of doctrine and classical evangelical unity has been compromised. If, as Ramm suggests, one's view of Scripture is so important, then a weakening of that view should concern us.

The issue of full or limited inerrancy is a serious one among those within the framework of historic evangelicalism. In the past a healthy and energetic spirit of cooperation has existed among evangelicals from various and diverse theological persuasions and ecclesiastical affiliations. Lutherans and Baptists, Calvinists and Arminians, and believers of all sorts have united in evangelical activity. What has been the cohesive force of that unity? In the first instance, there has been a consensus of catholic articles of faith, such as the deity of Christ. In the second instance, a strong point of unity has been the cardinal doctrine of the Protestant Reformation: justification by faith alone. In the last instance, there has been the unifying factor of *Sola Scriptura* in the sense of full inerrancy. The only "creed" that has bound the Evangelical Theological Society together, for example, has been the affirmation of inerrancy. Now that point of unity is in jeopardy. The essence of Christianity is not the issue. But a vital point of consistent evangelicalism is.[24]

SOLA SCRIPTURA AND LIMITED INERRANCY

Is *Sola Scriptura* compatible with a view of Scripture that limits inerrancy to matters of faith and practice? Theoretically it would seem to be possible if "faith and practice" could be separated from any part of Scripture. So long as biblical teaching regarding faith and practice were held to be normative for the Christian community, there would appear to be no threat to the essence of Christianity. However, certain problems exist with such a view of Scripture that do seriously threaten the essence of Christianity.

The first major problem we encounter with limited inerrancy is the problem of *canon reduction*. The canon or "norm" of Scripture is reduced *de facto* to that content relating to faith and practice. This immediately raises the hermeneutical question concerning what parts of Scripture deal with faith. As evangelicals wrestle among themselves in intramural debates, they must keep one eye focused on the liberal world of biblical scholarship, for the principle of the reduction of canon to matters of "faith" is precisely the chief operative in Bultmann's hermeneutic. Bultmann thinks we must clear away the prescientific and faulty historical "husk" of Scripture to get to the viable kernel of "faith." Thus, although Bultmann has no inerrant kernel or *kerygma* to fall back on, his problem of canon reduction remains substantially the same as that of those who limit inerrancy to faith and practice.

Before someone cries foul or cites the informal fallacy of *argumentum ad hominem* (abusive) or the "guilt by association" fallacy, let this concern be clarified. I am not saying that advocates of limited inerrancy are cryptic or even incipient Bultmannians, but that there is one very significant point of similarity between the two schools: *canon reductionism*. Evangelical advocates of limited inerrancy are not expected to embrace Bultmann's mythical view of New Testament supernaturalism. But their method has no inherent safeguard from an arbitrary delimitation of the scope of the biblical canon.

The second serious problem, closely related to the first, is the problem of the relationship of faith and history, perhaps the most serious question of contemporary New Testament scholarship. If we limit the notion of inerrancy to matters of faith and practice, what becomes of biblical history? Is the historical substratum of the gospel negotiable? Are only those portions of the biblical narrative that have a clear bearing on faith inerrant? How do we escape dehistoricizing the gospel and relegating it to a level of supratemporal existential "decision"? We know that the Bible is not an ordinary history book but a book of *redemptive* history. But is it not also a book of redemptive *history?* If we exclude the realm of history from the category of inspiration or inerrancy either in whole or in part, do we not inevitably lose the gospel?

The third problem we face with limiting inerrancy to matters of faith and practice is an apologetic one. To those critics outside the fellowship of evangelicals, the notion of "limited inerrancy" appears artificial and contrived. Limited inerrancy gets us off the apologetical hook by making us immune to religious-historical criticism. We can eat our cake and have it too. The gospel is preserved; and our faith and practice remains intact while we admit errors in matters of history and cosmology. We cannot believe the Bible concerning earthly things, but we stake our lives on what it says concerning heavenly things. That approach was totally abrogated by our Lord (John 3:12).

How do we explain and defend the idea that the Bible is divinely superintended in part of its content but not all of it? Which part is inspired? Why only the faith and practice parts? Again, which are the faith and practice parts? Can we not justly be accused of "weaseling" if we adopt such a view? We remove our faith from the arena of historical verification or falsification. This is a fatal blow for apologetics as the reasoned defense of Christianity.[25]

Finally, we face the problem of the domino theory. Frequently this concern is dismissed out of hand as being so much alarmism. But our doctrine of Scripture is not a child's game of dominoes. We know instances in which men have abandoned belief in full inerrancy but have remained substantially orthodox in the rest of their theology. We are also aware of the sad instances in which full inerrancy is affirmed yet the substance of theology is corrupt. Inerrancy is no guarantee of biblical orthodoxy. Yet even a cursory view of church history has shown some pattern of correlation between a weakening of biblical authority and serious defection regarding the *Wesen* of Christianity. The *Wesen* of nineteenth-century liberalism is hardly the gospel evangelicals embrace.

We have already seen, within evangelical circles, a move from limited inerrancy to challenges of matters of faith and practice.

When the apostle Paul is depicted as espousing two mutually contradictory views of the role of women in the church, we see a critique of apostolic teaching that does touch directly on the practice of the church.[26] In the hotly disputed issue of homosexuality we see denominational commissions not only supplementing biblical authority with corroborative evidence drawn from modern sources of medical psychological study but also "correcting" the biblical view by such secular authority.[27] The direction of these movements of thought is a matter of grave concern for advocates of full inerrancy.

We face a crisis of authority in the church. It is precisely our faith and our practice that is in question. It is for faith and practice that we defend a fully infallible rule—a total view of *Sola Scriptura.*

We know some confusion has existed (much unnecessarily) about the meaning of full inerrancy. But with all the problems of definition that plague the concept, we do not think it has died the death of a thousand qualifications.

We are concerned about *Sola Scriptura* for many reasons. But we affirm it in the final analysis not because it was the view of the Reformers, not because we slavishly revere Hodge and Warfield, not even because we are afraid of dominoes or a difficult apologetic. We defend it and express our deep concern about it because we believe it is the truth. It is a truth we do not want to negotiate. We earnestly desire dialogue with our evangelical brothers and colaborers who differ from us. We want to heal the wounds that controversy so frequently brings. We know our own views are by no means inerrant. But we believe inerrancy is true and is of vital importance to our common cause of the gospel.

Further dialogue within the evangelical world should at least help us clarify what real differences there are among us. Such clarification is important if there is to be any hope of resolving those differences. We do not intend to communicate that a person's Christian faith stands or falls with his view of Scripture. We do not question the Christian commitment of advocates of limited inerrancy. What we do question is the correctness of their doctrine of Scripture, as they question ours. But we consider this debate, as serious as it is, a debate between members of the household of God. May our Father bring us to unity here as he has in many glorious affirmations of his gospel.

Notes

[1]"Die einzige Quelle und Norm aller christlichen Erkenntnis ist die heilige Schrift," a statement in Heinrich Heppe, *Die Dogmatik der evangelisch-reformierten Kirche* (Neukirchen Kreis Moers: Neukirchener, 1958), p. 10.

[2]Harold J. Grimm, *The Reformation Era* (New York: Macmillan, 1954), p. 114.

[3]Gordon Rupp, *Luther's Progress to the Diet of Worms* (New York: Harper, 1964), p. 69.

[4]Paul Althaus, *The Theology of Martin Luther*, trans. Robert C. Schultz (Philadelphia: Fortress, 1966), pp. 6-7. Althaus cites Luther: "But everyone, indeed, knows that at times they [the fathers] have erred as men will; therefore, I am ready to trust them only when they prove their opinions from Scripture, which has never erred" (WA 7, 315; LW 32, 11). Also: "Hold to Scripture and the Word of God. There you will find truth and security—assurance and a faith that is complete, pure, sufficient, and enduring" (WA 7, 455; LW 32, 98).

[5]This is precisely the challenge raised by Hans Küng. He says, "The counter question to Protestant theology must be: Is it sufficient to replace the infallibility of the ecclesiastical teaching office with the infallibility of the Bible? Instead of the infallibility of the Roman pontiffs or of ecumenical councils, are we to have the infallibility of a "paper pope"? Küng's answer is clearly in the negative *(Infallible? An Inquiry,* trans. Edward Quinn [New York: Doubleday, 1971], p. 209).

[6]For a more thorough treatment of Luther's view of inerrancy see John Warwick Montgomery, "Lessons from Luther on the Inerrancy of Holy Writ," in *God's Inerrant Word* (Minneapolis: Bethany Fellowship, 1974). See also in the same volume J.I. Packer, "Calvin's View of Scripture."

[7]The confessional citations are taken from Arthur C. Cochrane, ed., *Reformed Confessions of the 16th Century* (Philadelphia: Westminster, 1966).

[8]Cf. French Confession, Art. II; Belgic Confession, Art. II; Second Helvetic Confession, Chap. XII; Westminster Confession, Chap. I. A further technical point may be added: General revelation is no less infallible than Scripture. The *sola* here refers to a unique source of infallible *written* revelation.

[9]H.J. Schroeder, *Canons and Decrees of the Council of Trent* (St. Louis: Herder, 1941), p. 17 (italics mine).

[10]G.C. Berkouwer, *Vatikaans Concilie en Nieuwe Theologie* (Kampen: Kok, 1964), p. 129.

[11]Ibid., pp. 110-12.

[12]*Haec porro supernaturalis revelation, secundum universalis Ecclesiae fidem a sancta Tridentina Synodo declaratam continetur "in libris scriptis et sine scripto traditionibus"*—Vatican I (Denzinger 1787). *Verum quoque est, theologis semper redeundum esse ad divinae revelationis fontes: eorum enim est indicare qua ratione ea quae a vivo Magisterio docentur, in Sacris Litteris et in divina "traditione," sive explicite, sive implicite inveniantur—Humani Generis* (Denzinger 2314).

[13]"Truth, Unity, and Peace," the Encyclical "Ad Petri Cathedram" of Pope John XXIII to the Entire Catholic World, *The Encyclicals and Other Messages of John XXIII* (Washington, D.C.: TPS, 1964), pp. 24ff.

[14]Bernard Ramm, "Is 'Scripture Alone' the Essence of Christianity?" in *Biblical Authority*, ed. Jack Rogers (Waco: Word, 1977), pp. 111-12.

[15]Ibid., p. 112.

[16]One important qualification must be added here. If a person were convinced that Jesus infallibly taught a particular view of Scripture and at the same time obstinately refused to affirm or submit to it, it would properly raise grave questions about the state of his soul.

[17]J.I. Packer, *"Sola Scriptura' in History and Today"* in *God's Inerrant Word,* ed. John Warwick Montgomery (Minneapolis: Bethany Fellowship, 1974), p. 44.

[18]Ibid., p. 43.

[19]Francis Schaeffer, "Form and Freedom in the Church" in *Let the Earth Hear His Voice*, ed. J.D. Douglas (Minneapolis: World Wide, 1975), pp. 364-65, cited by Richard Lovelace in his unpublished essay, "Limited Inerrancy: Some Historical Perspectives."

[20]Francis Schaeffer, *No Final Conflict* (Downers Grove, Ill.: InterVarsity Press, 1975), p. 13.

[21]Harold Lindsell, *The Battle for the Bible* (Grand Rapids: Zondervan, 1976), p. 139.

[22]Ramm, "'Scripture Alone' . . . ?" p. 122.

[23]Ibid., pp. 122-23.

[24]Though full inerrancy has been a rallying point for much evangelical cooperation, it would be incorrect to assert that historic evangelicalism has been monolithic in its view of Scripture. In many instances (such as in the Evangelical Theological Society) inerrancy has functioned as a strong point of unity. But I am not prepared to maintain that full inerrancy is the *Wesen* of (essential to) evangelicalism in the sense that one cannot be an evangelical if he rejects it. I regard limited inerrancy to be inconsistent with *Sola Scriptura* and detrimental to the cause of evangelicalism, but not the touchstone of evangelicalism itself.

[25]In a book dedicated to Rudolf Bultmann, Van Harvey makes this observation: "Of these many problems, none has caused more consternation and anxiety in the breasts and minds of Christian believers than the application of critical historical methods to the New Testament and, especially, to the life of Jesus. It is fashionable among contemporary Protestant theologians to consider this aspect of the problem something of a dead issue except, that is, among fundamentalists and other conservative Christians. My conviction is that this attribute is unwarranted, that even the most sophisticated theological programs of the last two or three decades have failed to grapple in any rigorous and clear fashion with the thorny issues created by a revolution in the consciousness of Western man of which critical historiography is but the expression" *(The Historian and the Believer* [New York: Macmillan, 1966], p. xi).

[26]Paul K. Jewett, *Man as Male and Female* (Grand Rapids: Eerdmans, 1975), pp. 112-35.

[27]See *Sexuality and the Human Community* (Philadelphia: Office of the General Assembly of the United Presbyterian Church in the U.S.A., 1970).

THE PREACHER AND GOD'S WORD

James Montgomery Boice

James Montgomery Boice is pastor of Tenth Presbyterian Church, Philadelphia, Pennsylvania, and speaker on the Bible Study Hour radio program heard weekly from coast to coast. He is a graduate of Harvard College, A.B.; Princeton Theological Seminary, B.D.; and the University of Basel, Switzerland, D.Theol. He served as assistant editor of Christianity Today *before becoming pastor of the Tenth Presbyterian Church in Philadelphia. Dr. Boice is the author of* Witness and Revelation in the Gospel of John; Philippians: An Expositional Commentary; The Sermon on the Mount; How to Really Live It Up; How God Can Use Nobodies; The Last and Future World; The Gospel of John *(5 vols.); "Galatians" in* The Expositor's Bible Commentary; Can You Run Away From God?; Our Sovereign God, *editor;* The Sovereign God; *and* God the Redeemer. *He is chairman of the Philadelphia Conference on Reformed Theology, and is on the Board of Directors of The Stony Brook School and Presbyterians United for Biblical Concerns.*

5 *James Montgomery Boice*

THE PREACHER AND
GOD'S WORD

ANYONE WHO thinks seriously about the state of preaching in the twentieth century must notice a strange contradiction. On the one hand, there is a strong acknowledgment of the need for great preaching, usually defined as expository preaching. But on the other hand, good expository preaching has seldom been at a lower ebb. Evangelical (and even liberal) seminaries exhort their young men, "Be faithful in preaching. . . . Spend many hours in your study poring over the Bible. . . . Be sure that you give the people God's Word and not merely your own opinions."[1] But in practice these admonitions are not heeded, and the ministers who emerge from the seminaries—whether because of poor instruction, lack of focus, or some other, undiagnosed cause—generally fail in this primary area of their responsibility.

Pulpit committees know this. So do the people who sit in the pews Sunday after Sunday. Many know what they want. They want a minister who will make his primary aim to teach the Bible faithfully week after week and also embody what he teaches in his personal life. But ministers like this from the standard denominations and even some others are hard to find and apparently are getting harder to find all the time. What is wrong? How are we able to explain this strange contradiction between what we say we want and what is actually produced by most of our seminaries?

DECLINE OF PREACHING

This problem is so obvious that a number of answers have inevitably been given, most of which contain some truth. One answer is that attention has been shifted from preaching to other needed aspects of the pastoral ministry: counseling, liturgics, small group dynamics, and other concerns. Hundreds of books about these diverse aspects of the ministry are appearing every year, many of them best sellers, but there are not many valuable books on preaching. There are some, but they are not very popular. And one cannot really imagine a work like Clarence Macartney's *Preaching Without Notes* attracting anywhere near the degree of attention in the seventies as it attracted just thirty years ago. Clearly the attention of a great majority of ministers is being directed away from expository preaching to other concerns.

On the surface, then, this seems to be a valid explanation of the decline of good preaching, and one might even tend to justify the decline temporarily if, so we might argue, these other equally important concerns are being rediscovered. But the trouble with this view is that these concerns need not be set in opposition to good preaching and, indeed, must not. In fact, the greatest periods of faithful expository preaching were inevitably accompanied by the highest levels of sensitivity to the presence of God in worship and the greatest measure of concern for the cure of souls.

The Puritans are a great example, though one could cite the Reformation period or the age of the evangelical awakening in England as well. The Puritans abounded in the production of expository material. We think of the monumental productions of men like Richard Sibbes (1577-1635), Richard Baxter (1615-1691), John Owen (1616-1683), Thomas Watson (d. 1686), John Flavel (1627-1691), Jonathan Edwards (1702-1758), and that later Puritan Charles Haddon Spurgeon (1834-1892). These men produced material so serious in its nature and so weighty in its content that few contemporary pastors are even up to reading it. Yet common people followed these addresses in former times and were moved by them. Worship services were characterized by a powerful sense of God's presence, and those who did such preaching and led such services were no less concerned with the individual problems, temptations, and growth of those under their care. Who in recent years has produced a work on pastoral counseling to equal Baxter's *The Reformed Pastor* (1656)? Who has analyzed the movement of God in individual lives as well as did Jonathan Edwards in *A Narrative of Surprising Conversions* (1737) and *Religious Affections* (1746) or Archibald Alexander in his *Thoughts on Religious Experience* (1844)? Questions like these should shake us out of self-satisfied complacency and show that we are actually conducting our pastoral care, worship, and preaching at a seriously lower level.

Another explanation given for the current decline in preaching is the contemporary distrust of oratory. Again, there is some truth to this. The decline in popularity of orators such as William Jennings Bryan has been accompanied by a decline in the popularity of oratorical preaching by men like Henry Ward Beecher and his more recent successors. But the trouble with this explanation is that great preaching is not inseparably wedded to any one style of preaching. Indeed, the Puritans themselves were not commonly great orators. And, for that matter, good speakers are not really unpopular today, though today's popular style is somewhat different from that of a previous age. John Kennedy was quite eloquent, for example, and he was highly regarded for it.

The trouble with these explanations of the decline of preaching is that each is based on an external cause. They deal with the mind-set of the secular world. What is really needed is an explanation that deals with the state of the contemporary church and with the mind-set of her ministers.

What is the answer in this area? The answer is that the current decline in preaching is due, not to external causes, but to a prior decline in a belief in the Bible as the authoritative and inerrant Word of God on the part of the church's theologians, seminary professors, and those ministers who are trained by them. Quite simply, it is a loss of confidence in the existence of a sure Word from God. Here the matter of inerrancy and authority go together. For it is not that those who abandon inerrancy as a premise on which to approach the Scriptures necessarily abandon a belief in their authority. On the contrary, they often speak of the authority of the Bible most loudly precisely when they are abandoning the inerrancy position. It is rather that, lacking the conviction that the Bible is without error in the whole and in its parts, these scholars and preachers inevitably approach the Bible differently from inerrantists, whatever may be said verbally. In their work the Bible is searched (to the degree that it is searched) for whatever light it may shed on the world and life *as the minister sees them* and not as that binding and overpowering revelation that tells us what to think about the world and life and even formulates the questions we should be asking about them.

Nothing is sadder than the loss of this true authority, particularly when the preacher does not even know it. The problem is seen in a report of a panel discussion involving a rabbi, a priest, and a Protestant minister. The rabbi stood up and said, "I speak according to the law of Moses." The priest said, "I speak according to the tradition of the Church." But the minister said, "It seems to me. . . ."[2]

It is hard to miss the connection between belief in the inerrancy of Scripture issuing in a commitment to expound it faithfully, on the one hand, and a loss of this belief coupled to an inability to give forth a certain sound, on the other. Dr. D. Martyn Lloyd-Jones is one who makes the connection. He writes on the decline of great preaching:

> I would not hesitate to put in the first position [for the decline]: the loss of belief in the authority of the Scriptures, and a diminution in the belief of the Truth. I put this first because I am sure it is the main factor. If you have not got authority, you cannot speak well, you cannot preach. Great preaching always depends upon great themes. Great themes always produce great speaking in any realm, and this is particularly true, of course, in the realm of the Church. While men believed in the Scriptures as the authoritative Word of God and spoke on the basis of that authority you had great preaching. But once that went, and men began to speculate, and to theorize, and to put up hypotheses and so on, the eloquence and the greatness of the spoken word inevitably declined and began to wane. You cannot really deal with speculations and conjectures in the same way as preaching had formerly dealt with the great themes of the Scriptures. But as belief in the great doctrines of the Bible began to go out, and sermons were replaced by ethical addresses and homilies, and moral uplift and socio-political talk, it is not surprising that preaching declined. I suggest that this is the first and the greatest cause of this decline.[3]

Lloyd-Jones is right in the main in this analysis. So our first thesis is that *the contemporary decline in great (expository) preaching is due in large measure to a loss of belief in biblical authority and that this loss is itself traceable to a departure from that high view of inspiration that includes inerrancy.*

WORD OR DEED?

But there is a problem at this point. The problem is that those who approach preaching in this way are accused of making the Bible their God and of centering the gospel in a book rather than in the divine acts of God in history, which is where it should be, according to their critics.

There are various forms of this latter perspective. On the one hand, there is a valuable emphasis on the specific "acts" of God. An example of this is the work of G. Ernest Wright entitled *The God Who Acts*. In this study Wright stresses the acts rather than the Word of God, saying, "The Word is certainly present in the Scripture, but it is rarely, if ever, dissociated from the Act; instead it is the accompaniment of the Act."[4] He points to the Exodus as the event on which the giving of the law is based (Exod. 20:1-3) and to the signs given to and by the prophets. According to Wright, it is the act that is primary. Another form of this critique is held by those who emphasize the revelation of God to the individual in such a way that personal experience rather than the Word of God becomes decisive. What should we say to these emphases? Are those who emphasize the Word in their preaching bibliolaters? Do they worship the Bible? Have they distorted the Bible's own teaching through their excessive veneration of it?

Not at all! It is true that the acts of God can be overlooked in a certain kind of preoccupation with linguistic and other textual problems. But this is more often the error of the Old or New Testament scholar than the preacher. Actually, a hearty emphasis on the Word of God is itself profoundly biblical, and it is even mandatory if one is to appreciate the acts of God prophesied, recorded, and interpreted in the Scriptures.

Which comes first, the word or the deed? The most common answer is the deed, which the word is then seen to interpret. But this is a distortion of the biblical picture. Certainly the acts of God are of major importance in the Bible and in Christian experience. But it is inaccurate to say that the deeds come first. Rather, the Word comes first, then the deeds, then a further interpretation of the deeds scripturally.

Let me give a number of key examples. First, the creation. It is possible to argue that God created the world initially and then interpreted the creation to us in the opening pages of the Bible and elsewhere. But this is not the way the Bible itself presents this matter. What Genesis says is that first there is God, after that the

Word of God, and then creation. God spoke, and after that the things about which God spoke came into being. The words "and God said" are the dominant feature of the opening chapter of Genesis (vv. 3, 6, 14, 20, 24, 26). Only after that does God "see" (vv. 4, 10, 12, 19, 21, 25), "separate" (vv. 4, 7), "call" (vv. 5, 8, 10), "make" (vv. 7, 16, 25), "set" (v. 17), "create" (vv. 21, 27), "bless" (vv. 22, 28), and explain to the first man and woman what he has done (vv. 28-30).

The second example is the call of Abraham, the next great step in the unfolding of God's purposes. There is nothing in Abraham's story to indicate that God acted in any particular way to call Abraham. We read rather, "Now the Lord *said* to Abram, 'Go from your country and your kindred and your father's house to the land that I will show you. And I will make of you a great nation, and I will bless you, and make your name great, so that you will be a blessing'" (Gen. 12:1, 2). It was after receiving this word of promise that "Abram went, as the LORD had told him" (v. 4). Faith in the divine promise characterized Abraham, and it is for his response to the Word of God, even in the absence of the deed, that Abraham is praised: "By faith Abraham obeyed when he was called to go out to a place which he was to receive as an inheritance; and he went out, not knowing where he was to go" (Heb. 11:8), "And he [Abraham] believed the LORD; and he reckoned it to him as righteousness" (Gen. 15:6; cf. Rom. 4:3; Gal. 3:6).

A third example of the primacy of the word to deed is the Exodus itself, so often cited in precisely the opposite fashion. Here we do have a mighty intervention of God in history on the part of his people, and it is certainly true that the ethical standards of the Old Testament are imposed on the grounds of this deliverance ("I am the LORD your God, who brought you out of the land of Egypt. . . . You shall have no other gods before me," Exod. 20: 2, 3). But this does not mean that the deed precedes the word. Rather the deliverance was fully prophesied beforehand to Abraham (Gen. 15:13, 14) and was announced to Moses as the basis on which he was to go to Pharaoh with the command to let God's people go (Exod. 3:7-10).

The same is true of the coming of Jesus Christ. This fourth example is the greatest illustration of the intervention of God in history. But the event was preceded by the word even here, through prophecies extending back as far as the germinal announcement of a future deliverer to Eve at the time of the Fall

(Gen. 3:15) and continuing up to and including the announcement of the impending birth to Zechariah the priest (Luke 1:17),
Joseph (Matt. 1:20-23), Mary (Luke 1:30-33), and others who
were looking for the redemption of Jerusalem (Luke 2:25-27,
36-38).

Emphasis on the word of God and faith in that word in reference to the coming of Christ is particularly evident in David's
great prayer in 2 Samuel 7. God has just established his covenant
with David, promising that his throne should be established
forever. David responded:

> Who am I, O Lord GOD, and what is my house, that thou hast
> brought me thus far? And yet this was a small thing in thy eyes, O
> Lord GOD: *thou hast spoken* also of thy servant's house for a great
> while to come, and hast shown me future generations, O Lord GOD!
> And what more can David say to thee? For thou knowest thy
> servant, O Lord GOD! Because of *thy promise*, and according to thy
> own heart, thou hast wrought all this greatness, to make thy
> servant know it. . . . And now, O LORD God, confirm for ever the
> word which thou hast *spoken* concerning thy servant and concern-
> ing his house, and do *as thou hast spoken;* and thy name will be
> magnified for ever, saying, 'The LORD of hosts is God over Israel,'
> and the house of thy servant David will be established before thee.
> For thou, O LORD of hosts, the God of Israel, hast made this
> revelation to thy servant, saying, 'I will build you a house'; there-
> fore thy servant has found courage to pray this prayer to thee. And
> now, O Lord GOD, thou art God, and *thy words* are true, and thou
> hast *promised* this good thing to thy servant; now therefore may it
> please thee to bless the house of thy servant, that it may continue
> for ever before thee; for thou, O Lord GOD, hast *spoken*, and with
> thy blessing shall the house of thy servant be blessed for ever (vv.
> 18-21, 25-29).

In these words David exercises faith in the word of God primarily.

A final example of the primacy of the word is Pentecost, which
inaugurated the present age of the church. Peter, who was the
spokesman for the other disciples on that occasion, recognized
immediately that this was nothing other than the fulfillment of
God's promise to Joel regarding a future outpouring of the Holy
Spirit. "Men of Judea and all who dwell in Jerusalem . . . these
men are not drunk, as you suppose, since it is only the third hour
of the day; but this is what was spoken by the prophet Joel: 'And in
the last days it shall be, God declares, that I will pour out my
Spirit upon all flesh, and your sons and your daughters shall

prophesy, and your young men shall see visions, and your old men shall dream dreams'" (Acts 2:14-17).

As the Bible presents the matter, in each of these key moments in the divine economy, the word of God rather than the deed of God is primary, though of course in some cases the actual writing of the biblical material followed both. This is not meant to suggest that the actual intervention of God is unimportant, for, of course, that is not true. It is of major importance. But it is meant to say that we are not getting the emphasis reversed when we follow the biblical pattern and stress the actual word or promise of God in contemporary preaching. This does not undermine God's acts. The promise is about them. It merely places them in the context in which God himself places them in Scripture.

So the second thesis is that *an emphasis on the Word of God in today's preaching is demanded by the very nature of God's revelation of himself in history.* It is declared of God through the psalmist, "Thou hast exalted above everything thy name and thy word" (Ps. 138:2).

BIBLICAL PREACHING

Having recognized the primacy of the word in God's own dealings with the human race, it is not at all difficult to note the primacy of the word in that early Christian preaching recorded in the New Testament.

Peter's great sermon given on the day of Pentecost is an example. Peter and the other disciples had experienced a visible outpouring of the Holy Spirit, manifested by the sound of a rushing mighty wind and tongues of fire that had rested on each of the disciples (Acts 2:1-3). They had begun to speak so that others heard them in a variety of languages (v. 4). In addition to this, they had all just been through the traumatic and then exhilarating experiences of the crucifixion, resurrection, visible appearance, and ascension of the Lord Jesus Christ. These were heady experiences. Yet when Peter stood up to preach on Pentecost, he did not dwell on his or anyone else's experiences, as many in our day might have done, but rather preached a profoundly biblical sermon centered on specific biblical passages. The format was as follows: First, there are three verses of introduction intended to link the present manifestations of the outpouring of the Spirit to God's prophecy of that even in Joel. These were a lead-in to the major text. Second, Peter cites the prophecy in Joel at length, giving a total of five verses to it. Third, there is a declaration of the guilt of the men of Jerusalem in Christ's death, which, however, was in full accordance with the plan and foreknowlege of God, as Peter indicates. This takes three verses. Fourth, there is an extended quotation from Psalm 16:8-11, occupying four verses. These stress the victory of Christ over death through his resurrection and exaltation to heaven. Fifth, there is an exposition of the sixteenth psalm, occupying five verses. Sixth, there is a further two-verse quotation from Psalm 11:1, again stressing the supremacy of Christ. Seventh, there is a one-verse summary.

Peter's procedure is to quote the Old Testament and then explain it and after that to quote more of the Old Testament and explain it, and so on. Moreover, the Scripture predominates. For although there are eleven verses of Scripture versus twelve for other matters, much of the material in the twelve verses is introductory to the Scripture and the rest is explanation.

Peter's procedure does not demand that every subsequent Christian sermon follow precisely the same pattern. We know that even the other New Testament preachers did not preach in the same way that Peter did; each rather followed a pattern determined by his own gifts and understanding. But the sermon does suggest the importance that Peter gave to the actual words of God recorded in the Old Testament and the concern he had to interpret the events of his time in light of them.

One chapter farther on we have another example of Peter's preaching. This time his outline was slightly different, for he began with a more extended statement of what God had done in Jesus Christ, in whose name the lame man had just been healed. But this quickly leads to the statement that all that had happened to Jesus had been foretold by God through the prophets (Acts 3:18) and then to two specific examples of such prophecy: Deuteronomy 18:18, 19 (cited in vv. 22, 23) and Genesis 22:18 (cited in v. 25). The burden of each of these sermons is not the current activity of God in Christ and/or the Holy Spirit alone, still less the subjective experience of such activity by Peter or the others. Rather it is the activity of God as proclaimed in the Scriptures: "God has promised to do these things, and he has done them. Now, therefore, repent and believe the gospel."

Peter was concerned to affirm that God had said certain things about the coming of Christ and the Holy Spirit, that he had said these in certain specific passages and words of the Old Testament, and that God was now fulfilling these promises precisely. In other words, in his preaching and thinking Peter gave full authority to the very words of Scripture as the words of God.

Peter's own formal statement of his attitude to the Word is in 2 Peter 1:19-21. "And we have the prophetic word made more sure. You will do well to pay attention to this as to a lamp shining in a dark place, until the day dawns and the morning star rises in your hearts. First of all you must understand this, that no prophecy of scripture is a matter of one's own interpretation, because no prophecy ever came by the impulse of man, but men moved by the Holy Spirit spoke from God."

In his discussion of this text and others like it, Dewey M. Beegle argues that since Peter was not in possession of the original autographs of Scripture and does not refer his statement to them explicitly, he is referring therefore only to errant copies and cannot be saying that they are inerrant in accordance with a specific theory of verbal inspiration. He concludes, "There is no explicit indication in this passage that Peter made any essential distinction between the originals and the copies. The important teaching is that the Scriptures had their origin in God; therefore the copies that Peter's readers had were also to be considered as being from God and thus worthy of their careful study."[5] But surely to argue that Peter did not believe in an inerrant Scripture in this way is merely to read a twentieth-century distinction into Peter's situation where it does not belong. Certainly Peter is *not* making a distinction between the originals and copies. That is just the point. He is not even thinking in these terms. If someone would point out an error in one of his copies, he would readily acknowledge it—obviously the error got in somewhere—but still say precisely the same thing: that is, that the Old Testament is God's Word in its entirety. It is "from God" (v. 21). Consequently, it is "more sure" even than the theophany that he and two other disciples had been privileged to witness on the Mount of Transfiguration (vv. 16-19).[6]

Peter is not the only one whose sermons are recorded in Acts, of course. Stephen is another. Stephen was arrested by the Sanhedrin on the charge of speaking "blasphemous words against [the law of] Moses and God," and he replied with a defense that occupies nearly the whole of Acts 7. This sermon contains a comprehensive review of the dealings of God with Israel, beginning with the call of Abraham and ending with the betrayal and crucifixion of Christ. It is filled with Old Testament quotations.

Its main point is that those who were defending the law were not obeying it. Rather, like those before them, they were resisting the Word of God and killing God's prophets (Acts 7:51-53).

Acts 13 marks the beginning of the missionary journeys of Paul and contains the first full sermon of Paul recorded. It is a combination of the kinds of sermons preached by Peter on Pentecost and Stephen on the occasion of his trial before the Sanhedrin. Paul begins as Stephen did, pointing out to the Jews of the synagogue of Antioch of Pisidia that God, who had dealt with the people of Israel for many years, had promised repeatedly to send a Savior, who has now come. He points out that this one is Jesus, whose story he briefly relates. Then he offers his texts, citing in rapid sequence Psalm 2:7 (Acts 13:33), Isaiah 55:3 (v. 34), and Psalm 16:10 (v. 35). These are explained, and then there is a concluding quotation from Habakkuk 1:5 (v. 41). Clearly the emphasis is on these verses.

On the next Sabbath in the same city many came together to hear this gospel, but the Jews were jealous and spoke against it. Paul responded by preaching a sermon on Isaiah 49:6, "I have sent you to be a light for the Gentiles, that you may bring salvation to the uttermost parts of the earth" (Acts 13:47).

So it is throughout the other sermons in Acts. The only apparent exception is Paul's well-known address to the Athenians, recorded in chapter 17. In this address the apostle begins, not with Scripture, but with quotations from the altars of the Athenians and from Greek poetry, and he never gets to Scripture. But one must remember that Paul's sermon was interrupted at the point at which he began to speak of the resurrection. Can we think that if he had been allowed to continue he would have failed to mention that this was in fulfillment of the Jewish Scriptures, as he did when he reached this same point in other sermons? Besides, even if he would not have quoted Scripture on this occasion, it would only mean that he departed from his normal prodecure. It would not mean that he regarded the very words of God, recorded in the Old Testament, less highly.

We conclude that each of the New Testament preachers is concerned to proclaim God's word as fulfilled in the events of his own lifetime. Moreover, his emphasis is on this word rather than on his own subjective experiences or any other less important matter. The thesis that emerges at this point, our third, is that *preaching that is patterned on the preaching of the apostles and other early witnesses will always be biblical in the sense that the very words of the Bible will be the preacher's text and his aim will be a faithful exposition and application of them.* This cannot be done if the preacher is sitting in judgment on the Word rather than sitting under it.

"HIGHER" CRITICISM

But how can the preacher honestly treat the Bible in this way in view of the development of biblical studies in the last century? We might understand how such an "uncritical" attitude would be possible for the early Christian preachers. They probably did not even consider the problem in adhering to an inerrant and therefore totally authoritative Bible when they actually had only "errant" copies to work from, for they did not know the full extent of the difficulties. But we do know. We "know" there are errors. We "know" that the Bible is not one harmonious whole but rather a composite work consisting of many different and often conflicting viewpoints. Is it not true that we must simply give up the biblical approach because of the assured findings of archaeology, history, and, above all, higher criticism? Are we not actually compelled to treat the Bible differently?

Our "knowledge" that the Bible contains errors and is a composite and often contradictory work is said to be the reason for the overthrow of the old inerrancy position. But is it? When looked at from the outside, this seems to be the reason. But confidence is shaken when we realize that most of the alleged errors in the Bible are not recent discoveries, due to historical criticism and other scholarly enterprises, but are only difficulties known centuries ago to most serious Bible students. Origen, Augustine, Luther, Calvin, and many others were aware of these problems. Yet they did not feel compelled to jettison the orthodox conception of the Scriptures because of them. Either they were blatantly inconsistent, which is a difficult charge to make of men of their scholarly stature, or else they had grounds for believing the Bible to be inerrant—grounds that were greater than the difficulties occasioned by the few problem passages or apparent errors.

What grounds could there be? The basic foundation of their belief, borne in upon them by their own careful study of the Bible and (as they would say) the compelling witness of the Holy Spirit to them through that study, was the conviction that the Scriptures of the Old and New Testaments are uniquely the Word of God and are therefore entirely reliable and truthful, as God is truthful.

Divine truthfulness was the rock beneath their approach to Scripture. Their study of the Bible led them to this conclusion, and thereafter they approached the difficulties of biblical interpretation from this premise.

This approach has characterized the majority of their heirs in the Reformation churches down to and including many at the present time, although not all inerrantists feel obligated to use this approach.[7] In fuller form, the argument has been presented as follows:

1. The Bible is a reliable and generally trustworthy document. This is established by treating it like any other historical record, such as the works of Josephus or the accounts of war by Julius Caesar.
2. On the basis of the history recorded by the Bible we have sufficient reason for believing that the central character of the Bible, Jesus Christ, did what he is claimed to have done and therefore is who he claimed to be. He claimed to be the unique Son of God.
3. As the unique Son of God, the Lord Jesus Christ is an infallible authority.
4. Jesus Christ not only assumed the Bible's authority; he taught it, going so far as to teach that it is entirely without error and is eternal, being the Word of God: "For truly, I say to you, till heaven and earth pass away, not an iota, not a dot, will pass from the law until all is accomplished" (Matt. 5:18).
5. If the Bible is the Word of God, as Jesus taught, it must for this reason alone be entirely trustworthy and inerrant, for God is a God of truth.
6. Therefore, on the basis of the teaching of Jesus Christ, the infallible Son of God, the church believes the Bible also to be infallible.[8]

The negative criticism of our day does not approach the Bible in this way. Rather, it approaches it on the premise of naturalism, a philosophy that denies the supernatural or else seeks to place it in an area of reality beyond investigation. It is this philosophy, rather than the alleged errors, that is the primary reason for rejection of the inerrancy position by such scholars.

Critical views of the Bible are constantly changing, of course, and at any one time they exist in a bewildering variety of forms. Currently we think of the Bultmannian school in Germany, the post-Bultmannians, the *Heilsgeschichte* school of Oscar Cullmann and his followers, and others. These views are competing. Nevertheless, there are certain characteristics that tie the various forms of higher criticism together.

One characteristic is that the Bible is considered man's word about God and man rather than God's word about and to man. We recognize, of course, that the Bible does have a genuine human element. When Peter wrote that "men moved by the Holy Spirit spoke from God," he taught that it is *men* who spoke just as surely as he taught that their words were from God. We must reject any attempt to make the Bible divine rather than human just as we reject any attempt to make it human rather than divine. But recognizing that the Bible is human is still a long way from saying that it is not uniquely God's word to us in our situation and *merely* human thoughts about God, which is what the negative higher criticism does. The view that the Bible is man's word about God is simply the old romantic liberalism introduced into theology by Friedrich D.E. Schleiermacher (1768-1834), namely that "the real subject matter of theology is not divinely revealed truths, but human religious experience," as Packer indicates.[9] Is this the case? The answer to this question will determine how and even if one can preach the Word of God effectively.

A second characteristic of much higher criticism is its belief that the Bible is the result of an evolutionary process. This has been most evident in Old Testament studies in the way the documentary theory of the Pentateuch has developed. But it is also apparent in Bultmann's form-criticism, which views the New Testament as the product of the evolving religious consciousness of the early Christian communities.

Again, we acknowledge that there is a certain sense in which God may be said to unfold his revelation to men gradually so that a doctrine may be said to develop throughout the Scriptures. But this is not the same thing as saying that the religious expressions of the Bible have themselves developed in the sense that the negative critical school intends. In their view, early and primitive understandings of God and reality give way to more developed conceptions, from which it also follows that the "primitive" ideas may be abandoned for more contemporary ones. Crude notions, such as the wrath of God, sacrifice, and a visible second coming of the Lord Jesus Christ, must be jettisoned. So may various aspects of church government and biblical ethics. If we decide that homosexuality is not a sin today, so be it. We can even cite the continuing activity of the Holy Spirit in revealing new truth to us in support of our rejection of such "outmoded" ethics. If we find Paul's strictures regarding the role of men and women in the government of the church obsolete, we can just disregard them. Such thoughts are blasphemous! Yet this is what flows from the essential outlook of today's higher criticism.

The third characteristic of much higher criticism follows directly upon the first two; namely, that we must go beyond the Scriptures if we are to find God's will for our day.

But suppose the preacher is convinced by the Scripture and by the authority of Christ that the Bible is indeed God's word to man rather than merely man's word about God, that it is one consistent and harmonious divine revelation and not the result of an evolutionary process, that it is to the Scriptures and not to outside sources that we must go for revelation. We must still ask: Can he actually proceed like this today? Is this not to fly in the face of all evidence? Is it not dishonest? The answer is: Not at all. His procedure is simply based on what he knows the Bible to be.

We may take the matter of sacrifices as an example. Everyone recognized that sacrifices play a large role in the Old Testament and that they are not so important in the New Testament. Why is this? How are we to regard them? Here the negative critic brings in his idea of an evolving religious conscience. He supposes that sacrifices are important in the most primitive forms of religion. They are to be explained by the individual's fear of the gods or God. God is imagined to be a capricious, vengeful deity. Worshipers try to appease him by sacrifice. This seems to be the general idea of sacrifice in the other pagan religions of antiquity. It is assumed for the religion of the ancient Semite peoples too.

In time, however, this view of God is imagined to give way to a more elevated conception of him. When this happens, God is seen to be not so much a God of capricious wrath as a God of justice. So law begins to take a more prominent place, eventually replacing sacrifice as the center of religion. Finally, the worshipers rise to the conception of God as a God of love, and at this point sacrifice disappears entirely. The critic who thinks this way might fix the turning point at the coming of Jesus Christ as the result of his teachings. Therefore, today he would disregard both sacrifices and the wrath of God as outmoded concepts.

By contrast, the person who believes the Bible to be the unique and authoritative Word of God works differently. He begins by noting that the Old Testament does indeed tell a great deal about the wrath of God. But he adds that this element is hardly eliminated as one goes on through the Bible, most certainly not from the New Testament. It is, for instance, an important theme of Paul. Or again, it emerges strongly in the Book of Revelation, where we read of God's just wrath eventually being poured out against the sins of a rebellious and ungodly race. Nor is this all. The idea of sacrifice is also present throughout the Scriptures. It is true that the detailed sacrifices of the Old Testament system are no longer performed in the New Testament churches. But this is not because a supposed primitive conception of God has given way to a more advanced one, but rather because the sacrifice of Jesus Christ of himself has completed and superseded them all, as the Book of Hebrews clearly maintains. For this person the solution is not to be found in an evolving conception of God, for God is always the same—a God of wrath toward sin, a God of love toward the sinner. Rather, it is to be found in God's progressing revelation of himself to men and women, a revelation in which the sacrifices (for which God gives explicit instructions) are intended to teach both the dreadfully serious nature of sin and the way in which God has always determined to save sinners. The sacrifices point to Christ. Therefore John the Baptist, using an integral part of ancient Jewish life that all would understand, is able to say, "Behold, the Lamb of God, who takes away the sin of the world" (John 1:29). And Peter can write, "You know that you were ransomed from the futile ways inherited from your fathers, not with perishable things such as silver or gold, but with the precious blood of Christ, like that of a lamb without blemish or spot" (1 Peter 1:18, 19).

In this the data is the same. The only difference is that one scholar approaches Scripture looking for contradiction and development. The other has been convinced that God has written it and therefore looks for unity, allowing one passage to throw light on another. The Westminster Confession put this goal well in saying, "The infallible rule of interpretation of Scripture is the Scripture itself; and therefore, when there is a question about the true and full sense of any Scripture, it must be searched and known by other places that speak more clearly" (1, ix).[10]

The thesis that emerges from this discussion is that *higher criticism does not make the highest possible view of the Scripture untenable.*

On the contrary, higher criticism must be judged and corrected by the biblical revelation.

REGENERATION

Not only does God exalt his name and his very words in the Scriptures and likewise in the preaching of that Word, but he also exalts his Word in the saving of men and women. For it is by his Word and Spirit, and not by testimonies, eloquent arguments, or emotional appeals, that he regenerates the one who apart from that regeneration is spiritually dead. Peter states it thus: "You have been born anew, not of perishable seed but of imperishable, through the living and abiding word of God" (1 Peter 1:23).

There are many moving images for the Word of God in the Bible. We are told in the Psalms that the Bible is "a lamp" to our feet and "a light" to our path (Ps. 119:105). Jeremiah compares it to "a fire" and to "a hammer which breaks the rock in pieces" (Jer. 23:29). It is "milk" to the one who is yet an infant in Christ (1 Peter 2:2) as well as "solid food" to the one who is more mature (Heb. 5:11-14). The Bible is a "sword" (Heb. 4:12; Eph. 6:17), a "mirror" (1 Cor. 13:12; James 1:23), a "custodian" (Gal. 3:24), a "branch" grafted into our bodies (James 1:21). These are great images, but none is so bold as the one Peter used in this passage: the Word is like human sperm. Peter uses this image, for he wishes to show that it is by means of the Word that God engenders spiritual children.

In the first chapter Peter has been talking about the means by which a person enters the family of God. First, he has discussed the theme objectively, saying that it is on the basis of Christ's vicarious death that we are redeemed. "You know that you were ransomed from the futile ways inherited from your fathers, not with perishable things such as silver and gold, but with the precious blood of Christ, like that of a lamb without blemish or spot" (vv. 18, 19). Second, he has discussed the theme subjectively, pointing out that it is through faith that the objective work of Christ is applied to us personally. "Through him you have confidence in God, who raised him from the dead and gave him glory, so that your faith and hope are in God" (v. 21). Finally, having mentioned these truths, Peter goes on to discuss the new birth in terms of God's sovereign grace in election, this time showing that we are born again by means of the Word of God, which he then likens to the male element in procreation. The

Vulgate makes this clearer than most English versions, for the word used there is *semen*.

What does this teach about the way in which a man or woman becomes a child of God? It teaches that God is responsible for the new birth and that the means by which he accomplishes this is his living and abiding Word. We might even say that God does a work prior to this, for he first sends the ovum of saving faith into the heart. Even faith is not of ourselves, it is the "gift of God" (Eph. 2:8). Afterward, when the sperm of the Word is sent to penetrate the ovum of saving faith, there is a spiritual conception.

The same ideas are in view in James 1:18, which says, "Of his own will he brought us forth ['begot he us,' KJV] by the word of truth that we should be a kind of first fruits of his creatures."

The point of these verses is that it is by means of the very words of God recorded in the Scriptures and communicated to the individual heart by the Holy Spirit that God saves the individual. It is as Calvin says, in speaking of faith:

> Faith needs the Word as much as fruit needs the living root of a tree. For no others, as David witnesses, can hope in God but those who know his name (Ps. 9:10). . . . This knowledge does not arise out of anyone's imagination, but only so far as God himself is witness to his goodness. This the prophet confirms in another place: "Thy salvation [is] according to thy word" (Ps. 119:41). Likewise, "I have hoped in thy word; make me safe" (Ps. 119:4, 40, 94). Here we must first note the relation of faith to the Word, then its consequence, salvation.[11]

Is it really the Word that God uses in the salvation of the individual? If it is, if God chooses so to operate, then the preacher can hardly fail to give the words of God the fullest measure of prominence in his preaching. He will revere them as that supernatural gift without which nothing that he desires to see happen within the life of the individual will happen.

We conclude that *the texts of the Bible should be preached as the very (and therefore inerrant) Word of God if for no other reason than that they are the means God uses in the spiritual rebirth of those who thereby become his children.*

A FORK IN THE ROAD

It is often said by those who adhere to inerrancy that a departure from the orthodox view of the Scripture at this point inevitably leads to a decline in adherence to orthodox views in other areas. This would no doubt be true if all deviators were consistent, but it is hard to demonstrate that this is *always* true, since one individual is not always as rigorous in carrying out the full implications of a position as another. It is enough to say that this has happened enough times with those who have entered the ministry to concern deeply anyone who sincerely desires the stability and growth of evangelicals and evangelical institutions.

On the other hand, and this is perhaps even more significant, many of those who have wrestled through the problem of the Bible's inerrancy or noninerrancy and have come out on the inerrancy side, testify to this as the turning point in their ministries, as that step without which they would not have been able to preach with the measure of power and success granted to them by the ministration of the Holy Spirit. I can testify that this has been true in my own experience. As pastor of a church that has seen many hundreds of young men go into the ministry through years of seminary training, I can testify that this has been the turning point for the majority of them as well. It is sometimes said by those who take another position that inerrantists have just not faced the facts about the biblical material. This is not true. These men have faced them. But they are convinced that in spite of those things that they themselves may not fully understand or that seem to be errors according to the present state of our understanding, the Bible is nevertheless the inerrant Word of God, simply because it is the Word of God, and that it is only when it is proclaimed as such that it brings the fullest measure of spiritual blessing.

May God raise up many in our time who believe this and are committed to the full authority of the Word of God, whatever the consequences. In desiring that "Thus saith the Lord" be the basis for the authority of our message, the seminaries, whether liberal or conservative, are right. But we will never be able to say this truthfully or effectively unless we speak on the basis of an inerrant Scripture. We are not in the same category as the prophets. God has not granted us a primary revelation. We speak only because others, moved uniquely by the Holy Spirit, have spoken. But because of this we do speak, and we speak with authority to the degree that we hold to what Charles Haddon Spurgeon called "the *ipsissima verba*, the very words of the Holy Ghost."[12]

We need a host of those who have heard that Word and who are not afraid to proclaim it to a needy but rebellious generation.

Notes

[1]The author's own theological training was received at Princeton Theological Seminary, a seminary hardly noted today for being strongly evangelical, though many of its students are. But in the homiletics department the greatest honor was given to expository preaching and the students were repeatedly urged to allow nothing to take the place of solid exegetical work in sermon preparation. The problem is that the admonitions are not followed by the vast majority of Princeton's graduates, and the reason for this is that the concerns of the homiletics department are being undercut by the views of the Bible conveyed in the biblical departments.

[2]Of course, Judaism and Roman Catholicism are also undergoing their own struggles with the question of authority. The anecdote must involve an orthodox rabbi, a tradition-oriented priest, and an average Protestant clergyman.

[3]D. Martyn Lloyd-Jones, *Preaching and Preachers* (Grand Rapids: Zondervan, 1971), p. 13. Lloyd-Jones also cites a reaction against "pulpiteering" (in which he is thinking along lines similar to my remarks about oratory) and "publication of sermons" as literary productions.

[4]G. Ernest Wright, *God Who Acts* (London: SCM, 1952), p. 12. In more recent writing Wright has broadened this view considerably, stressing that a biblical Act is not merely a historical happening but rather one in which the Word of God is also present to interpret and give it meaning (cf. *The Old Testament and Theology* [New York: Harper, 1969], p. 48).

[5]Dewey M. Beegle, *Scripture, Tradition, and Infallibility* (Grand Rapids: Eerdmans, 1973), p. 155.

[6]A clear example of the fallacy of this kind of argument is Beegle's similar treatment of the often quoted words of Augustine to Jerome, "I have learned to pay them [the canonical books] such honor and respect as to believe most firmly that not one of their authors has erred in writing anything at all" (Epistle 82, *The Fathers of the Church*, vol. 12, "St. Augustine: Letters 1-82," trans. Wilfrid Parsons [Washington, D.C.: The Catholic University of America Press, 1951], p. 392). Beegle disregards this statement because we know: 1) that Augustine read the Bible in a Latin translation made from the Septuagint, 2) that this version was errant, and 3) that Augustine was therefore wrong in regarding it so highly *(Scripture, Tradition, and Infallibility*, p. 137). But Augustine was no fool at this point. He knew there were errors in the various translations and copies. In fact, his letter goes on to say, "If I do find anything in those books which seems contrary to truth, I decide that either the text is corrupt, or the translator did not follow what was really said, or that I failed to understand it." Still Augustine says that the Bible, as God's Word, can be fully trusted. He believed that, as originally given, it was an inerrant revelation, and the copies (except where it can be shown that errors in text or translation have crept in) can be regarded and quoted as those inerrant originals.

[7]Some simply accept the Bible for what it claims to be and then operate on that premise. Thoughtful exponents of this view feel that any other approach is unwarranted and even presumptuous if the Bible is truly God's Word ("If it is, how can we presume to pass judgment on it?").

[8]This classical approach to the defense of Scripture is discussed at length by R.C. Sproul in "The Case for Inerrancy: A Methodological Analysis," in *God's Inerrant Word*, ed. John Warwick Montgomery (Minneapolis: Bethany Fellowship, 1974), pp. 248-60. It is the element most lacking in Earl Palmer, "The Pastor as a Biblical Christian," in *Biblical Authority*, ed. Jack Rogers (Waco: Word, 1977). Palmer speaks of a fourfold mandate given by Jesus Christ to every Christian: to grow in our relationship with God, to love our neighbor, to share the gospel, and to build up the body of Christ (p. 127). But as true and important as these four items are, they do not express the whole of our obligation as Christians. We are to believe and follow Christ in *all* things, including his words about Scripture. And this means that Scripture is to be for us what it was to him: the unique, authoritative, and inerrant Word of God, and not merely a human testimony to Christ,

however carefully guided and preserved by God. If the Bible is less than this to us, we are not fully Christ's disciples.

[9]J.I. Packer, *"Fundamentalism" and the Word of God* (Grand Rapids: Eerdmans, 1960), p. 148.

[10]I discuss the higher criticism at greater length in *The Sovereign God* (Downers Grove, Ill.: InterVarsity, 1978), pp. 97-109. The preceding five paragraphs are borrowed from pp. 113-15.

[11]John Calvin, *Institutes of the Christian Religion,* ed. John T. McNeill, trans. Ford Lewis Battles (Philadelphia: Westminster, 1960), Vol. 1, pp. 576, 577.

[12]Charles Haddon Spurgeon, *Lectures to My Students* (Grand Rapids: Zondervan, 1954), p. 73.

EVANGELICALS AND THE DOCTRINE OF INERRANCY

Kenneth S. Kantzer

Kenneth S. Kantzer is Professor of Biblical and Systematic Theology and Vice-President and Dean of Trinity Evangelical Divinity School, and Editor of Christianity Today. *He is a graduate of Ashland College, B.A.; Ohio State University, M.A.; Faith Theological Seminary, B.D., S.T.M.; and Harvard University, Ph.D. He has also studied at the University of Goettingen, Germany, and the University of Basel, Switzerland. Before coming to Trinity in 1963, he was for many years chairman of the division of Bible, philosophy, and Christian education at Wheaton College. He has taught at Gordon College, Gordon-Conwell Divinity School, and King's College. Dr. Kantzer has written chapters in numerous publications, including* Religions in a Changing World, The Evangelicals, Inspiration and Interpretation, The Word for This Century, *and* Jesus of Nazareth: Savior and Lord. *He is editor of* Evangelical Roots. *He has served as consulting editor of* His *magazine and was book review editor for the* Journal of the Evangelical Theological Society. *He is a member of the American Theological Society and the Evangelical Theological Society, having served as president of the latter organization. For a short time he held a pastorate in Rockport, Massachusetts.*

6 *Kenneth S. Kantzer*

EVANGELICALS AND THE DOCTRINE OF INERRANCY

E VANGELICALISM HAS gained in visibility and newsworthiness during recent years, and the reason is clear: Evangelicals have returned to the offensive.

Whereas nonevangelical seminaries are barely holding their own by admission of large numbers of women students, the inclusion of many M.A. and Ph.D. candidates who have little or no intention of seeking ordination to the ministry, and the introduction of the new Doctor of Ministry degree, evangelical schools are everywhere overflowing. Even after allowance is made for many of these same changes in their own programs, the evangelical schools are clearly attracting more students because of their evangelical position. Apart from works on psychology, the occult, sex, marriage, and the family, nonevangelical publishers are finding it difficult to market religious books by nonevangelical writers. But evangelical publishers are prospering today, so that many older publishing houses, which have long discouraged evangelical representation in their trade, are now openly courting evangelical writers and audiences.

The alternatives to evangelicalism, by contrast, have not fared well. The historicism[1] and rationalism of liberal theology have not proved religiously effective, and religious liberalism, at least in its traditional forms, seems everywhere in decline. Barthians, who brought so much promise to the theological scene in the late 1940s

147

and 1950s, never really caught on in the United States, and, with the misnamed and ill-fated death-of-God movement, simply faded out in the 1960s. In Europe Barthian theology dissolved before our eyes to be replaced by the cold winds of Bultmann and a new rationalism.

The theological world of the 1970s, therefore, by default if for no better reason, is interested in hearing what evangelicalism has to say—just at a time when evangelicals have recouped some of their early losses and are endeavoring once again to move into the open forum of religious debate. With this reentrance of evangelicalism on the theological battlefield has come a corresponding new influence from nonevangelicals and, indeed, some casualties among the evangelical forces.

Probably the most emotion-stirring issue on the current scene is that of the precise nature of biblical authority and particularly of biblical inerrancy, together with the question as to how we are to use the Bible in order to build a valid and normative theology. This is particularly the issue of the moment for evangelicals, though, of course, it has never been far from the center of their concern.

For the defenders of biblical inerrancy, it is significant that in this renewed battle over the Bible no new facts about the Bible have caused the issue to reappear in focus. The opponents of a high view of the Bible turn in the final analysis not to new discoveries in science or history or to new data in psychology or astrophysics. Rather, as in liberal proponent Harold De Wolf's *Theology of the Living Church* they list a series of contradictions between one biblical passage and another as final proof for scriptural errancy.[2] Likewise, among the evangelicals, Dewey Beegle does exactly the same with his blue-ribbon argument against inerrancy drawn from the apparent discrepancies between Kings and Chronicles and other biblical passages containing parallel references.[3] Such data was threshed over in detail by Jerome and Augustine in their correspondence sixteen centuries ago.[4] The medievalists, Luther and Calvin and their sons and daughters in the Reformation churches, and orthodox scholastics of the seventeenth, eighteenth, and even nineteenth centuries renewed the debate.[5] The newness of the issue of inerrancy is therefore not in any new fact but in a new way of looking at the data and in revived and heightened contemporary concern over the inspiration of the Bible.

PRESCRIPTION FOR THE FUTURE

I should like to propose some guidelines for evangelicals to enable them, while keeping themselves under the judgment of all of Scripture, to develop an effective strategy for action with reference to the doctrine of inerrancy.

1. Evangelicals never again dare withdraw from the intellectual battlefield of the day and hope thus to protect their delicate faith from worldly attack. Such anti-intellectualism is irresponsible. Not only does it lead inevitably to loss of faith, but there is something inherently antibiblical and anti-Christian about such an ego-protecting stance. It is a reflection of little faith. Moreover, it is inconsistent with the commands of the Lord to the church to go into all the world preaching and teaching and to let the light of the gospel shine out into the cultures of all people.

2. Inerrancy, the most sensitive of all issues to be dealt with in the years immediately ahead, should not be made a test for Christian fellowship in the body of Christ. The evangelical watch-cry must be "believers only, but all believers."[6] Evangelicals did not construct the church and do not set its boundaries. Christ is Lord, and he is Lord over his church. The bounds of fellowship, therefore, are to be set by Christ. They are determined by our relationship to Christ and by the life we share in him by grace through faith alone. The question is frequently raised: "Can one be an evangelical and not believe in inerrancy?" In answer, it is important to note that a word means what a significant body of those who use the word mean when they employ it. Since obviously not all use the word *evangelical* uniformly to mean the same thing, we must conclude that the word means several things and that even the same person does not always use it to mean the same thing. Words change their meanings by debasement or enrichment.

Several distinct meanings for the word evangelical can be documented. On the basis of its derivation, it refers in its broadest meaning to all who hold to the good news that sinful men and women are saved solely by the grace of God through faith in Jesus Christ.

Historically, a second meaning of the term has evolved. Because of the characteristic unity of doctrine espoused and defended by the early Protestants—whether Lutheran, Reformed, Anglican, or Anabaptist—the word evangelical has tended in a narrower sense to denote all who remain fully committed to Protestant orthodoxy. No one has ever been able to maintain a distinct boundary between the broad and the narrow usage. Accordingly, history reflects considerable disagreement as to how many departures a Christian believer can make and at what points before he ceases to be evangelical in the narrow sense but, if evangelical at all, remain so in the broad sense. Thus, a wide spread of divergent views is vaguely referred to as evangelical.

Finally, in dependence on its narrow meaning, the term sometimes refers merely to churches and movements originally characterized by orthodox Protestant or evangelical theology irrespective of whether or not the body continues to adhere to traditional evangelical doctrine. Examples are the Lutheran Church in northern Germany, Protestantism in South America, and Anglican low churches in England and some other parts of the English-speaking world.

Disregarding the last or institutional definition of the word, evangelical is, therefore, frequently used in a broad sense to denote full commitment to orthodox Protestantism.

One who rejects a doctrine characteristic of traditional Protestant orthodoxy such as, for example, the Virgin Birth or the inerrancy of Scripture, may defend himself by arguing that that particular doctrine is not really an essential element of traditional Protestantism. Or he may defend his evangelicalism by appealing to the broader definition—he really does believe in the essential gospel—the "evangel" of Christianity. But there is value in resisting the debasement of verbal coins and immense value in identification with one's cultural and religious roots. I am indisposed to relinquish the word *evangelical* to suborthodox viewpoints.

Nevertheless, in the interests of effective communication, where context does not precisely indicate the meaning intended, we must be content with a rather loose term that can mean different things to different people, or else tighten up our own expressions by the use of qualifying modifiers such as, on the one hand, "basically" evangelical, "generally" evangelical, or "essentially" evangelical and, on the other hand, "strictly" (which can refer to life style rather than to doctrine or experience), "conservatively" or "consistently" evangelical. However, even such carefully qualified terms carry a measure of ambiguity, for we ask: How strict, how conservative or consistent, in what way? Whenever it is important that the term be understood precisely and exactly, all who employ it must depend on context and qualifiers to indicate the sense in which they are using the word.

3. Though the doctrine of inerrancy should not be made a test for Christian fellowship and cannot be presumed to be included in the term evangelical as sometimes used, inerrancy, nevertheless, is important. It is even essential for *consistent* evangelicalism and for a full Protestant orthodoxy. This is why many evangelical institutions, such as the Evangelical Theological Society, include a statement on biblical inerrancy in their doctrinal platform and why many denominations require commitment to inerrancy for their officers and for ordination to the Christian ministry. This is a wise safeguard in view of the specific purpose of the group or individuals for whom it is required. To remove the word *inerrancy* from the platform of the Evangelical Theological Society, for example, would be to remove its *raison d'etre*. To fail to require belief in the inerrancy of Holy Scripture on the part of its leadership would be to jeopardize the evangelical heritage of a strict orthodoxy. But this guideline regarding the importance of requiring belief in inerrancy for certain purposes must not be substituted for the previous guideline that it should not be made a requirement for fellowship.

To the charge, sometimes made, that this introduces a double standard into the body of Christ, we must respond that only this conforms to the explicit instruction of Scripture provided for the church. Officers responsible for the guidance and instruction of the church must meet special requirements, including sound doctrine and firm adherence to the sure Word (Titus 1:9), but the church is composed of all who confess Christ as Lord and Savior regardless of the level of their doctrinal understanding. The evangelical church, by and large, has not required belief in inerrancy for fellowship (that is, for membership in the local church or for common worship), but it has traditionally demanded it of those entrusted with the leadership of the church or with teaching responsibilities.

4. The case for inerrancy rests precisely where it has always rested, namely, on the lordship of Christ and his commission to the prophets and apostles, who were his representatives. Because it rests on Christ and his authority, the question of inerrancy will therefore remain a key doctrine of the evangelical church so long as Christ is Lord. Evangelicals must remember, however, that this basis must be set forth anew for every generation. What was

adequate for Gaussen, Pieper, and Warfield is still valuable, but it is not necessarily adequate to serve as the foundation for the thinking of our generation. The case for inerrancy must be made anew with each presentation of the gospel teaching.

5. There is an imminent danger of a debilitating division within evangelical ranks over this issue and even of a decimation of evangelical forces. In the interest of truth and for the sake of obedience to the gospel, some of this may be necessary. When it is necessary, so be it. Clear and difficult distinctions must be set forth in love even when they will lead to unwanted misunderstanding and division. But some of the danger to evangelicalism is due only to dust in the air, and a little cool-headed sprinkling with cold water may clear the atmosphere.

6. Evangelicals must show that inerrancy is not a new doctrine, but conversely they must not concentrate so exclusively on inerrancy in their study and publishing as to make it *seem* to be the focus of the gospel or the central and fundamental doctrine of Christian faith, thus replacing Christ. Such a move would create a warped and unattractive image of Christianity and alienate many, not because they see objections to the doctrine of inerrancy, but because they see that it is not the gospel.

7. The presuppositions of the opponents of a full-fledged orthodoxy must be spelled out explicitly, and these must be set forth in contrast to sharply and clearly delineated presuppositions of evangelical faith. Before the facts are examined, many contemporary thinkers have predetermined their conclusions on the basis of nonbiblical positions taken as to theism, the supernatural, the nature of truth, the possibility of knowledge, the use of language, and other highly mooted philosophical and theological tenets. Invalid assumptions fundamentally inconsistent with biblical faith must be exposed as such. In their place must be substituted valid presuppositions, inherently consistent with each other and with clear biblical teaching.

8. Inerrancy must be defined carefully, and the entire church must be instructed without fear that such precise definition will weaken faith. Sometimes a weak faith must be destroyed in order to make room for a genuine and stronger faith. But the day is long past when evangelicals can refuse to face up to difficult arguments in their public writings on the grounds that they do not wish to give free hearing to a doctrine of demons. Extreme caution of this sort is born of little faith and in the end renders the youth and

lay Christians in our churches helpless before the innuendos and counterarguments that they hear in spite of us.

9. Evangelicals must show that they are not insisting on a single word as a shibboleth but rather are witnessing to the complete truthfulness and complete divine authority of Scripture. The terms infallibility, entire trustworthiness, plenary inspiration, inerrancy as to teaching, or inerrant in all it affirms, are all adequate. But all can be and are being used with qualifications suggesting only limited truthfulness and limited divine authority in Scripture, and thus the very opposite of what was originally intended. They are used to teach that some of what Scripture says, affirms, or teaches is *not true*.

The word *inerrancy* is also by no means free from such abuse and ambiguity. As applied to biblical inspiration, it is used by some to mean: a) exact and precise language throughout the whole of Scripture, b) literal interpretation of Scripture, or c) dictation methodology for the production of Scripture—all excesses of the right. According to others, inerrancy means: a) that the Scripture is certain to accomplish its purpose, b) that Scripture will never lead us astray from the gospel, or c) that Scripture is infallible only in limited areas such as its formal didactic passages or in those parts representing divine revelation—all excesses of the left. Evangelicals assert the truthfulness and divine authority of all Scripture, but this will need clarification and amplification.

10. Evangelicals must show the relevance of inerrancy thus defined. Inerrancy does not involve us in a useless defense of "Bible X," the unknown Bible that no one has ever seen, will ever see, or ever expects to see. Rather, evangelicals must show that it is just because we believe the autographs were inerrant that we have an objective path to truth. Assurance that we possess the correct text (on the basis of the objective and public data of textual criticism), plus assurance that we possess the meaning of the Scripture (on the basis of the objective and public data of grammar, syntax, and usage), provides proper and adequate support for the conviction that we have the truth of God. Such textual and exegetical data warrant complete certitude that we possess God's very truth in our Bibles.

11. Evangelicals must relate their doctrine of inerrancy to current biblical scholarship. Most heresies grow out of firm but one-sided grasping for truth. Consistent evangelicals must discover the piece of truth that gives strength to such basically

antievangelical methodologies as redaction criticism. But they must also be sufficiently alert and expert to draw the fine lines that inevitably distinguish truth from error. Old and New Testament experts should concentrate on the exposition of Scripture. In recent decades many evangelicals have been pushed by their doctoral mentors into linguistic studies and historical analysis but have carefully avoided expositions of Scripture that set forth its teaching in all richness. Now, by contrast, they must assume a proper responsibility to their Lord and to the church for the employment of their expertise in aiding in the construction of evangelical doctrine. Any Old or New Testament expert who seriously says, "I am not interested in biblical doctrine," ought immediately to question the state of his own evangelicalism. He should remember the ultimate purpose and significance of the Bible as set forth in 2 Timothy 3:15-17: "The sacred writings . . . are able to instruct you for salvation through faith in Christ Jesus. All scripture is inspired by God and profitable for teaching, for reproof, for correction, and for training in righteousness, that the man of God may be complete, equipped for every good work."

A FINAL WORD

Finally, a word seems appropriate both to those who as evangelicals defend the doctrine of biblical inerrancy and to those who as evangelicals do not rest at ease with the word *inerrant*. To those who confess their evangelical faith but are not at ease with inerrancy, I would point out three things:

1. Do not think you will win liberal and neoorthodox theologians to evangelicalism by fighting what you consider to be the bad view of the Bible held by more conservative evangelicals.

2. Proceed constructively as evangelicals, if you are evangelical. It is always easier to tear down than it is to build anew. Your first and primary responsibility as theologians is to build the instruction of our Lord into a meaningful whole, a positive body of doctrine and ethical guidance.

3. Since it is hard to think of an instance in which an institution has preserved complete doctrinal orthodoxy for as long as a full generation except on the basis of inerrancy, those who deny inerrancy ought to create an abiding and permanent institution that will maintain orthodoxy without it, before they commend their position on Scripture to the church. Limited inerrancy is a difficult line to draw. Let those who argue for a limited inerrancy

prove just once that they and their institutions can remain on that thin knife edge.[7]

For the consistent evangelical who witnesses to and defends the inerrancy of Holy Scripture I have this to say:

1. As evangelicals we must reverse our traditional role if we wish an effective strategy for our day. For seventy years we have been Green Berets furiously waging a rear-guard mission to search and destroy the enemy. We must stop conceiving of ourselves primarily as embattled guerrillas on the defensive. We must see ourselves primarily as heralds and persuaders.

2. If in order to show the importance of adhering to inerrancy we use the illustration of a row of dominos (and, with proper precautions, it is legitimate to do so), let us not forget that it is only an illustration and therefore must not be pressed at all points. There is, for example, nothing of mechanical inevitability by which an individual or institution that moves to an errancy view of the Bible must necessarily reject all orthodox doctrines. By his Spirit God can stay and has stayed the process. At times he has even reversed it. So it is worthwhile to try by all means to persuade our fellow believers of the truth and value of a doctrine of inerrancy. We should seek by every honorable means to penetrate and reclaim institutions that are wavering on this issue.

3. Evangelical strategy must incorporate a multidimensional perspective that is adequately comprehensive. Accordingly, evangelicals must not permit those who waffle on inerrancy to set the agenda for evangelical action, and especially they must not permit them to determine the way to present the case for biblical authority. Evangelicals must emphasize a full-fledged orthodoxy, including (but not focusing on) a doctrine of biblical inerrancy, for only in this way may Christianity be perceived in rounded fullness with the lordship of Jesus Christ set forth in full consistency and practical adequacy.

4. Conservative evangelicals, especially, must take great care, lest by too hasty a recourse to direct confrontation they edge into unorthodoxy the wavering scholar or student troubled either by problems in the biblical text or by some of the common connotations of the word *inerrant*. It is right to bend every effort to win to a right understanding of biblical inerrancy all who by any means are winnable, and anyone who takes with adequate seriousness the lordship of Jesus Christ is certainly winnable or should be presumed to be winnable.

In all that we do let us remember that orthopraxis is the crown of orthodoxy. Let us debate in love—with liberals in such a way that, if our love does not shine through our discourse, we lay down our pen, and with our fellow evangelicals deemed less consistent than ourselves, with honesty. Honesty—intellectual and spiritual no less than financial—is not a policy; anything less is wrong. As we defend what we believe to be our Lord's instruction as to the inerrancy of biblical authority, we are not out to conquer and destroy. Rather, we are witnesses seeking to share, convince, and persuade fellow believers in Christ to follow him in this as in all other areas of obedience to his written Word.[8]

Notes

[1]Historicism means many things, but as used here the term refers to the belief that ultimate meaning may be derived from a study of history, usually interpreted naturalistically.

[2]L. Harold De Wolf, *A Theology of the Living Church* (New York: Harper, 1953), pp. 68-74.

[3]Dewey M. Beegle, *Scripture, Tradition, and Infallibility* (Grand Rapids: Eerdmans, 1973), pp. 175-97.

[4]Augustine, *Letters* in *The Fathers of the Church*, trans. Wilfrid Parsons (Washington, D.C.: The Catholic University of America, 1951), 12:98-99, 411 and *passim*.

[5]See John F. Walvoord, *Inspiration and Interpretation* (Grand Rapids: Eerdmans, 1956); and Robert Preus, *The Inspiration of Scripture: A Study of the Theology of 17th-Century Lutheran Dogmaticians* (Edinburgh: Oliver and Boyd, 1955).

[6]See, for example, Arnold T. Olson, *Believers Only: An Outline of the History and Principles of the Free Evangelical Movement in Europe and North America* (Minneapolis: Free Church Publications, 1964). For the traditional Reformed view, note also statements by that arch defender of orthodoxy, Charles Hodge, in his *Systematic Theology* (New York: Scribner, 1872), 3:545-46. He says that the church requires only "a credible profession of faith," which he defines later as "a profession against which no tangible evidence can be adduced" (ibid., p. 625).

[7]I am not suggesting, of course, that one ought to believe in inerrant inspiration because it is advantageous to the church to do so. Rather, we ought to believe it because we seek to be obedient to our Lord. Inerrancy is important because of the stress Scripture itself lays on its own complete truthfulness and divine authority and also because of the role this doctrine has played in the church.

[8]This chapter is an edited reprint of a chapter entitled "Evangelicals and the Inerrancy Question" in *Evangelical Roots*, ed. Kenneth S. Kantzer (Nashville: Thomas Nelson, 1978).

INDEXES OF
NAMES, SUBJECTS, AND TITLES

INDEX OF
SCRIPTURE REFERENCES